THE
CRAFTSMAN
WOODTURNER

THE CRAFTSMAN WOODTURNER

PETER CHILD

 Sterling Publishing Co., Inc. New York

Published in 1984 by STERLING PUBLISHING CO., INC.
Two Park Avenue, New York, N.Y. 10016

Published in Great Britain by BELL & HYMAN LIMITED
First published in 1971 by G. Bell & Sons Ltd

Reprinted 1973, 1974
1976, 1977, 1979, 1981
New edition 1984
Reprinted 1987

Phototypeset by Tradespools Limited, Frome, England
Printed by BAS Printers, Over Wallop, Hampshire, England
Bound by Hunter & Foulis Limited, Edinburgh, Scotland

ISBN 0 8069 7882 1

Published by arrangement with Bell & Hyman Ltd
This edition available in the United States, Canada and the
Philippine Islands only

Contents

III. Appendix

List of Illustrations

The frontispiece was kindly supplied by Forestry magazine

Preface

A reliable well-worn route to becoming a craftsman is to serve under a master, becoming proficient by copying and following his example, listening to his explanations and advice, and working under his supervision.

Another, much more difficult road is the lonely one, no one at hand to instruct, demonstrate, or give patient replies to interminable questions as and when they arise. Success by this route is earned by dogged perserverance and sheer hard work, but only if coupled with a determination not to be beaten. This is 'the hard way'.

A book is only a substitute for the living instructor, but the author, having himself travelled the hard road and still remembering his early frustration and difficulties, has tried his utmost to give as much assistance as the written work can accomplish. As a craftsman, he has made a living; as a teacher, which came much later, he has taught thousands the basic principles of his craft, and the reader has cause to thank these pupils, since they have repeatedly asked the questions that this book endeavours to answer.

The first section describes all the main tools and techniques used in woodturnery. The second section consists of instructions for making a selection of typical examples of what woodturnery can produce. Full details of the techniques involved in making these projects are covered in the first part of the book.

There are few diagrams, because however carefully drawn it has been found from experience that they still are capable of misinterpretation. Studio photographs are also rare for the same reason. Wherever possible, the photographs have been taken in the workshop, and of the tools actually performing their function. The action has been stopped at the point best illustrating their purpose.

I am grateful to the late Mr Edwin W. Luker, F. Coll.H., Editor of the journal *Practical Education*. Without his gentle urging and unobtrusive skilled editing, this book would be unfinished. Mr K. W. Peck, inventor of the 'Flexicramp' contributed valuable information and photographs in connection with laminated turnery, and the Editors of *Practical Woodworking*, *Wordworker* and *Woodworking Crafts* gave their kind permission for inclusion of articles already published.

Introduction

Woodturning has been my business for many years. It is also my vocation. In 1963 I set up the first ever two-day residential courses in woodturnery, which I still run, teaching a maximum of two people at a time. My guests have come from all walks of life, all professions and trades, working and retired. I like teaching them all and we always part good friends – possibly because they all come with a common interest in wood and craftsmanship. Distance seems no object—they arrive from all parts of Britain and overseas.

My work in turning out products for sale has long been discontinued, and our family interests now lie in supplying the turner with every conceivable item that he or she may need. We are particularly interested in the development of new tools, chucks and methods of turning. Many of these are designed by my son Roy, and are included in this new edition.

The wrong approach to woodturning starts way back with the manufacturers of turning tools. Woodturning began as a highly specialist craft and only gained its widespread popularity as a hobby with the invention of the small electric drill and lathe attachment. A set of miniature tools accompanied these mini-lathes—which were useless—but the sheer novelty caught on, and interest grew in more practical lathes, thereby creating a need for proper tools. This sudden increase in interest put unexpected new demands on the tool manufacturers and the enthusiastic beginner often found the tools available were unsuitable or out of date. When I started I was fortunate enough to be given my first tools by the late Frank Pain, an eminent woodturner, an enthusiastic teacher, and a gentleman of the old school. Some of the tools he gave me were not even catalogued by any toolmaker. People who had to rely on standard tools were less well provided for. However since the first edition of this book was published in 1971 there have been great advances and improvements. The latest innovation, the result of long investigation and research by my son Roy, is the design and manufacture of accurately made, engineered, hand woodturning tools in high-speed steel. The days of carbon tool steel for turning tools are almost over.

Woodwork is taught in most schools, and invariably the woodwork department includes a wood lathe, yet often no instruction is provided for this machine. Many woodwork teachers are not properly qualified to teach the quite different skill of woodturnery, despite the great revival of interest in the craft. As a result, amateurs have been taught bad habits by other amateurs, and have given authority to the same bad habits and incorrect use of tools. This book aims to start from the beginning, and teach all the woodturning skills needed to create a well crafted piece of work, following teaching methods that have been tried and tested over many years.

A newcomer to the craft may have the opinion that all a lathe can do is make round objects, and that once the basic turnings such as a plate, a bowl, a lamp base, an egg cup and a chair leg have been achieved, then lathework becomes routine and routine becomes monotony. This is quite untrue. I have a widely assorted store of turned work and I enjoy the impact of seeing it dawn on people that woodturning can offer so much scope.

A fascination of the craft is the continuous discovery of new applications, the subtle blending of strong and gentle curves into new shapes as the machine is busily engaged in 'making things round'. Appearance can be transformed immediately by a deft cut with gouge and chisel, made either on purpose or occasionally by happy accident. A new concept can be conjured up when you have to remove the traces of a crack, knot or dig-in, and the result can turn out far better than your original theme.

The desire to make something is an almost automatic follow up of an interest in wood. But for the beginner it is often accompanied by a frustrated belief that he is incapable of original design. Many technical writers earn an honest living by supplying ideas for things to make, complete with measurements, scale drawings and photographs. The copyist can then borrow the mind of the originator and perhaps this is the best way to start. Later on, when handling a gouge becomes as natural as holding a pencil is to an artist, the copying becomes less and less important. The beginner finds he can picture some slight change of shape in his mind and can instantly reproduce it in the moving wood. It is then that the original feeling of frustration begins to melt away and an artist craftsman is born.

Old Hyde, Little Yeldham, Halstead, Essex
1984

PART I

PRINCIPLES
OF
TURNING

1. *Early lathe with wooden bed.* Converted to electric power drive and still producing work.

1. The Woodturning Lathe

These are machines on which wood can be fixed in such a manner that it can be revolved and fashioned into shapes by the use of tools applied to the moving surface. Earlier lathes were powered by human energy, employing such aids as twisted cord, springy saplings, treadmill, or foot treadle. The advent of steam power brought machines propelled by endless belts, and now we have electricity, but the principles of woodturnery remain unaltered from the very beginning.

Small but efficient lathes can be built by using the modern variable speed power drills fitted with the attachments available to convert them into woodturning machines. Constant speed drills often run too fast for good work, but speed reducers can be obtained to rectify this fault. This sort of lathe is only suitable for small projects, nut bowls, candlesticks, egg cups and table lamp bases, but it is inexpensive and a good introduction to what can turn out to be a fascinating hobby.

A lathe most useful for the keen enthusiast who may want to combine pleasure with business, is one powered by a motor at least of ¾ h.p.—should be capable of swinging a wood disc for a bowl 4″ deep and 12″ diameter on the outside (rear face turning) spindle, and a length of wood 4″ diameter and 2′ 6″ long between centres (spindle turning). My American friends call rear turning operations 'outboard' turnery—as good a description as any!

For school use, since the larger and heavier the machine the more safety factors available, or for the professional woodturner who wants big capacity and the weight and rigidity required for most efficient work, a machine capable of turning a bowl 5″ deep by 18″ diameter, and between centres a length of wood 6″ diameter by 3′ 0″ long, powered by a 1 h.p. motor, is the most suitable.

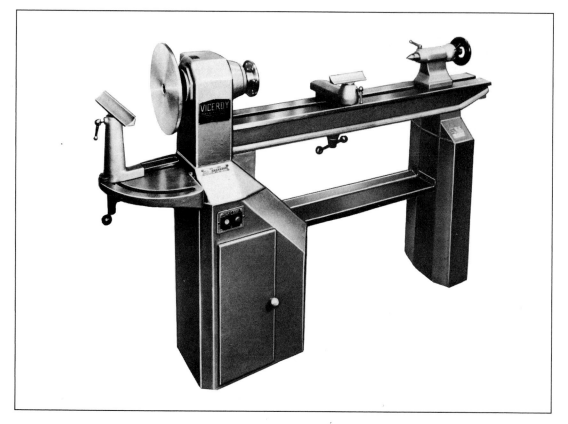

2. *Viceroy woodturning lathe.*
By courtesy Denford Machine Tools Ltd, Brighouse, Yorkshire.

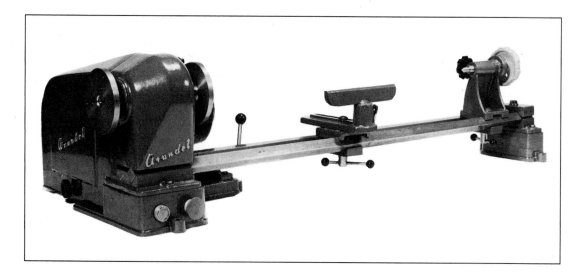

3. Arundel M230 lathe. (*Photograph courtesy of Treebridge Ltd*).

4. *Myford lathe.* One of my machines is of this make, and the cabinet stand has been packed with loose building bricks to obtain maximum steadiness for the largest work within its capacity. By courtesy Myford Engineering, Beeston, Nottingham.

Medium-sized lathes are usually bored to take No. 1 Morse Taper fittings, larger ones using No. 2.

A lightweight machine or heavier one that is badly sited, will be subject to vibration when running, and this is not conducive to good turnery of any description.

Machines on timber floors would be better situated where joists run underneath them, i.e. not parallel to them. 'Bounce' can be transmitted from floorboards right through the bed of the lathe and to the work. My Myford, although firmly on a concrete floor, has its stand additionally weighted down with bricks. Belt and pulley driven machines should be checked for correct belt alignment and tension, and there should be no play in the bearings. A fault in the Myford can arise due to the loosening of one or both grubscrews holding the pulley to the lathe spindle, so the pulley 'clacks' back and forth on the flats of the spindle. Similarly, the pulley keyed to the motor spindle can sometimes work loose, causing the same fault. There should be sufficient drive to the belt by just the weight of the motor, so no pressure should be needed on the motor to increase the distance between it and the headstock pulleys.

Pulley Speeds

As many different speeds up to four is desirable, but the highest for turning wood need not exceed 2,300 r.p.m. and even this is seldom required. A low speed in the region of 700 r.p.m. or lower still is best for large bowl turnery.

Stands

If the lathe obtained is not on its own stand it should be fitted to a specially made bench with legs braced both ways and of no less than 3″ × 3″ wooden stock or ¼″ angle iron. The bed for the lathe should be of wood at least 1″ thick.

Lathes in Craftrooms

Education authorities rightly impose stringent safety precautions, and machines obtained for schools should have incorporated every possible safety feature, such as completely enclosed drives, with all adjustments and locks easy to operate without the need for spanners.

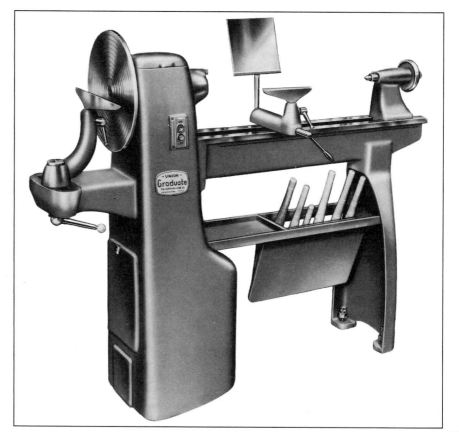

5. *Union Graduate lathe.* By courtesy T. S. Harrison & Sons Ltd, Heckmondwike.

2. Drilling in the Lathe

For some projects, drilling is essential, in others it may help to save time and ensure better accuracy. If it is at all possible the job should be set up so that the wood revolves while a stationary drill is fed into it. This makes for cleaner and better holes than the reverse procedure. There are a number of types of drill or bit suitable for use in lathes.

Engineers' (Morse) Twist Drills for Metalwork

Some of these are available ending in a morse taper shank that fits into the head or tailstock spindle, but more commonly they just have a straight shank and must be used in a chuck which has a morse taper fitting in its end. A chuck capable of holding up to ½″ diameter shank is the most useful. The drills are made for making holes in metal but are suitable for wood provided they are frequently withdrawn from the hole and the flutes freed from clogging wood swarf.

Long Hole Auger Boring for Lamp Bases

If a hollow centre guide and support is used in conjunction with this auger there should be no difficulty in boring accurate holes the complete length of the auger or double the length if the wood is reversed. It helps considerably if the shell portion is held uppermost when drilling so that the chips are collected in its 'basin', and the auger should be withdrawn very frequently to clear these chips so that the tool is not choked and burnt.

Carpenter's Centre Bits for Hand Brace

These have a gimlet screwpoint nose and a squared tang that fits into a hand brace. They have to be modified for lathe use and so that they can be held in a chuck the squared tang is cut off with a hacksaw. The thread of the nose point should deliberately be blunted or completely removed by filing away. The pulling action of the threaded point, so useful in hand work, is not required when used in a lathe and if left can 'snatch' when being fed into the work. This type of bit is comparatively cheap and will give good service provided the lathe is run at low speed so as not to cause overheating. A smoking bit is a sure sign of bluntness or excessive speed.

Saw Tooth Machine Centre Bits

This is a bit very much recommended for lathe work, and can also bore holes at an angle, overlapping, or at close centres. The holes are smooth and clean in any type of wood and accomplished with minimum power consumption. The bits do not choke in use and are easily sharpened. They are my favourite bits for most drilling jobs in the lathe.

Flatbits

These are designed for high speed drilling in wood. They have a spade type cutting head, and the shank has a three-flat section around which the chuck jaws should engage and be tightened for maximum hold. The comparatively long pyramid point is the drill's only guide and this should be brought up and slightly into the wood before the lathe is switched on; when drilling is completed the lathe should be switched off and the drill allowed to come to rest before it is withdrawn. This is especially important if it is necessary to bore the hole completely through the wood.

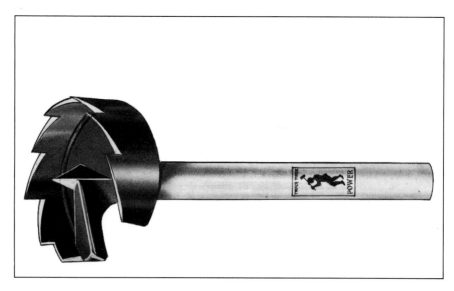

6. Saw tooth machine centre bit.

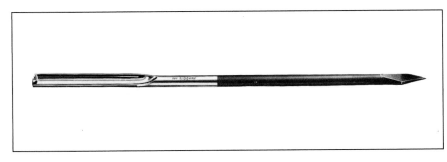

7. A long hole-boring auger.

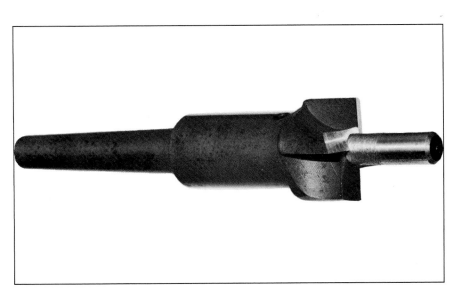

8. The counterbore drill. A most useful tool for lamp-bases—it can act as a drill, a four-prong drive, and can accurately centre turned pieces for joining up.

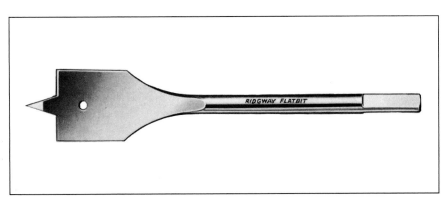

9. Machine boring flat bit.

3. Reversing Rotation in the Wood Lathe

One of the most valuable aids to good finishing is to be able to reverse the rotation of the motor and therefore work on the wood in two directions. However sharp the cutting or scraping tool, they invariably tend to lay the wood fibres down in the direction of cut, except when working against the grain as in making a bowl, where the two rough areas are always a beginner's headache. A 'finished' area may look and feel silken smooth to the touch in one direction, but a much rougher surface can be detected if stroked by the fingers the other way.

To run a single phase electric motor in 'reverse' does not harm it in any way, but the installation of a suitable switch that will do this should be left to a competent electrician. The diagram shows a typical method of wiring a 4-pole change-over switch (centre position off). In this system the reversing function is accomplished by the left-hand switch contacts. The starting and running windings are interchangeable at the switch, and with the switch stalk knob at the centre-off position, power is cut off from both windings whether the lathe starter is on or off. This is a useful safety factor. The switch frame, especially if metal, is earthed, also for safety reasons.

When the headstock spindle is running in reverse, the screw threads can no longer be depended upon to hold the faceplate securely, and a thick leather washer between faceplate boss and spindle shoulder can do much to ensure that the faceplate does not unscrew in reverse rotation. If the faceplate is put on tight enough to compress this washer there should be enough friction to enable light sanding or scraping to be done safely. Another method is to drill and tap the boss of the faceplate so that a grub screw can find a hold on the lathe spindle.

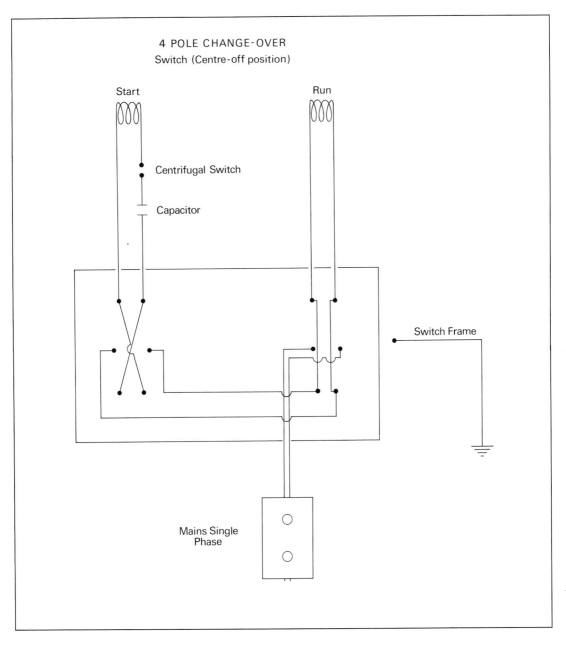

4 POLE CHANGE-OVER
Switch (Centre-off position)

Start

Run

Centrifugal Switch

Capacitor

Switch Frame

Mains Single
Phase

10. Wiring for 4-pole change-over switch.

It is possible on the Myford lathe, to take off and reverse the rest assembly collar so that the hand-rest can be positioned for work on the wood in reverse, but a separate free-standing rest can be made 'music stand fashion' from heavy tubing on tripod legs, or set into a base made from an oil drum filled with concrete for stability.

4. Bowl Turning: Outside Work

Work on a lathe can be roughly divided into two separate parts. There is turning between centres (spindle turnery), and bowl turning which is usually better carried out at the end of the lathe where there is no bed to hinder the correct use of the tools.

The tools used for the two types of work are, again roughly, of different types and section. For example, a spindle gouge cannot be used to best effect in the making of a bowl. A bowl gouge *can* be used for work between centres but only seldom takes the place of the right spindle gouge.

The biggest test of a good turner is his bowl-turning ability, and many beginners, having started woodturning between centres and without proper guidance, develop such bad habits in tool work that they are completely unable to make a bowl that is free from blemish. Speed of working may not be important to those who are interested in the craft purely as a hobby, but for guidance, a beautiful finished and polished bowl a foot in diameter and 3″ deep can be completed by a craftsman turner, using the right tools and correct methods, in not much over the hour.

A question usually asked of me by my student turners, especially if they are completely new to the craft, is 'What is the best wood suitable for me to start making a bowl?' It is so difficult to give a specific answer that I do not even try. Wood of any variety in any stage of dryness can be worked on the lathe with all kinds of results. Two pieces of wood from the same tree can be totally different in ease of working and finished appearance. Wood from a tree that has just been felled has a very high moisture content and is then often called 'wet', or 'green'. Until the moisture has been dried out, either naturally by stacking the boards and allowing climatic conditions to do the work (air-drying), or hastening this by artificial processes (kiln-drying), the wood is unseasoned. When the moisture content has been considerably reduced, say to 10%, we can then call the timber dry and seasoned.

Green timber is softer and correspondingly easier to turn, but will warp and twist out of shape as it seasons. On the other hand, wood can in certain circumstances get too dry, imparting a 'dead' feeling to the turner, and the cutting tool removes dusty fragments instead of cool shavings. More information on wood is given in chapter 30.

Because, on the whole, green timber is easier to work, we can turn this to good advantage, especially in the early stages of practice with tools, and we can employ methods that will overcome the misshapen result of the natural drying out processes. The use of tools is the same whether working on wet or dry timber—it is only the delay in the finishing methods that makes the difference. A timber that I can recommend with confidence is elmwood. Much maligned as cross-grained, liable to warp and twist, fungus afflicted, coarse and pithy in grain patches, it has immensely attractive variations in the grain even if the sections used are from the same plank. Its faults can be avoided and then the result is a very fine material that rewards the time and care spent on it.

Three common varieties used to be generally available, English 'red', fairly crisp cutting and some beautiful wild figure or 'flower'; Dutch elm, brown, rather featureless in grain, but mild cutting and easy to finish; wych elm, lighter in colour, green streaks, much harder to work and finish, but lovely to look at. As usual with home-grown hardwoods, most elm is air-dried and subject to the rule-of-thumb one inch of thickness per year. In these days of business economics and expensive storage space it is very easy to receive 'prime dry' elm which is really nothing of the sort, and when turned this can twist viciously and disappointingly. Fungus, which attacks unseasoned elm, will disappear from sight when almost dry, but the damage done to the fibres re-appears on the finished turning in the form of small 'corky' patches almost impossible to finish and polish cleanly. Filling the grain with wood-filler, so useful in flat work to repair and hide blemishes, very seldom works on turnery; the final polish seems to emphasise the repair rather than conceal it. Now Great Britain has been cursed by an epidemic of Dutch Elm Disease, causing death to many thousands of these beautiful trees. Good elm is becoming an exotic timber.

Warping and twisting in turned work, specially in hollow ware, is not completely due to moisture content. When large quantities of material are suddenly taken out of a disc of wood to leave the inside of a bowl, material that up to now has remained undisturbed, it is not surprising that the surround reacts adversely to the shock. An abdominal operation, whether one be 18 or 80, causes some doubling-up in most humans! I have some cherry which is known to be at least 15 years air dried, and the 2″ stuff can be seen twisting while still on the lathe and undergoing this operation. To obtain perfect results, it is recommended that any bowl, in whatever state of dryness, is 'rough-turned' to an even thickness throughout, leaving enough timber for finishing later. The bowl is left for a time depending on its initial dry state, to get over the shock before being replaced on the lathe and finished-turned.

It is not generally known that wood discs of large diameter, for example a 10″ diameter bowl, cannot satisfactorily be turned in one operation, whatever the type of wood or degree of seasoning. The release of stresses caused by the new shape will invariably force the wood to move, and the object will very soon be no longer round. Even timber that has been known to be dry for years will do this, so for permanent results it has to be turned over-size and over-thick, then left for as long as possible before being turned to finished shape.

Coming back to the virtues of elm as bowlwood, the ideal is to obtain the wood as 'wet' (unseasoned) as possible, straight from the saw in fact.

It should also be 'free from heart', 'free from large knots', 'free from sapwood'. You will not get it free as far as money is concerned—if you can, let me know. For bowlwork it is disced and rough-turned to a fairly even thickness of a one inch wall. This of course reduces air-drying time to one year, but another advantage of elm is that it is fairly quick-drying anyway, and the year can be further reduced to three months if the rough-turned work is left in airing cupboard temperature. Any fungus will not have had time to develop and all warping, twisting and 'doubling-up' will have been completed by then.

Rough-turning is fine practice in using a deep-fluted long and strong bowl-turning gouge. The wood is softer, the liquid sap keeps the tool cool and so retains its edge longer. Very heavy cuts can be taken and curled shavings fly all over the place, together with a free shampoo. Being in business as well as teaching, time is of the essence, and my favourite weapon is a ¾″ long and strong deep-fluted monster which can rough out a 4″ disc, 12″ diameter in under five minutes. The ⅜″ is the 'popular' model, but my students soon like to get familiar with the heavier ½″ which is almost as easy to control.

A properly ground and bevelled bowl-turning gouge will, upon being given proper starting instructions, carry on by itself and complete the cut almost entirely on its own. Digging-in and similar mishaps that frighten the instructor and pupil alike only occur with a badly shaped tool in the hands of a 'driver' who lacks knowledge of the basic principles of gouge control and therefore literally 'forces' the gouge to misbehave itself. My favourite

11. Side view of a brand-new long and strong carbon steel bowl-turning gouge as supplied from the manufacturer, slightly pointed and with a longer bevel than required.

12. The new gouge is ground straight-across and the bevel is correspondingly reduced to a thicker angle.

13. Top view of gouge showing the edge ground straight-across.

14. End view showing the comparative shallowness of a normal gouge used for turning between centres and unsuitable for bowlwork.

15. End view of long and strong, deep fluted bowl-turning gouge. The deep hollow is important.

students are those who have not had the chance to misuse a gouge, who in fact may never have seen one before, and who do exactly as I say, displaying no astonishment whatsoever when the gouge removes a beautiful thick shaving with a contented hiss of metal against wood. An example of where ignorance is bliss? On the other hand, someone who in the past has got used to forcing the tool and has incurred its sudden and violent reaction, retains the memory deeply and is nervous of a repetition.

The 'long and strong' is a heavy, solid tool, with metal where it counts and where needed for control. It appears logical that delicate work requires delicate instruments and it is common to assume that this follows in woodturnery, but this can be wrong. Consider that in bowl-turning, the wood, although circular, is not going round in a smooth flow of motion. Technically, the motor driving the pulleys is not going round smoothly either. Wood is not of the same density throughout, there is hard and soft and end grain all turning round together. No matter how heavy the lathe, vibration results in a greater or lesser degree. The edge of a tool held against all this is therefore receiving a multitude of 'knocks' and a fragile edge is not going to last very long. The new gouges from my manufacturer come to a slight nose point and the bevel is a trifle too long. Sharpened as they come, without a second bevel, the pointed nose is always in the way as the gouge moves across the timber in a proper cut, and the acute bevel takes too fragile an edge, so the first job is to grind the gouge edge straight across, which process removes the point and also shortens the original bevel. An angle of 45 degrees has been suggested as the ideal bevel, but I prefer one slightly longer. Since the gouge will not cut sweetly unless all the bevel is kept rubbing on the wood it is easy to slightly lift a short bevel off the wood without realising it, and a scraping cut results which dulls the edge and also leaves a rougher surface on the wood.

The deep fluting of a long and strong gouge robs the shaving of its strength by curling it down the flute, so that the shaving has no force to deflect the gouge from its proper path. A shallow gouge suitable for spindle turning (between centres) is not a good tool for bowl-work and the more a deep fluted tool looks like a 'U' the better.

My own technique is to sharpen the gouge on the edge of a 6″ diameter by 1″ dry carborundum wheel running at about 3,000 r.p.m., grinding right up to the edge of the tool so that it is taken direct to the wood without any oilstoning. An extremely keen burr-edge can be obtained this way if certain precautions against burning the metal are taken.

There are numerous grades of grindstones, some hard, some soft, and I like a grit combination coded by Carborundum Ltd. as A54-N5-V30W. This happens to be the grade supplied in a 6″ × 1″ wheel on Myford M.L.8 lathes. The stone must be kept free from all shine, since this means that some of the grit has worn smooth, still adheres to the wheel but does no cutting. To continue to grind a tool on this surface means pressure and any

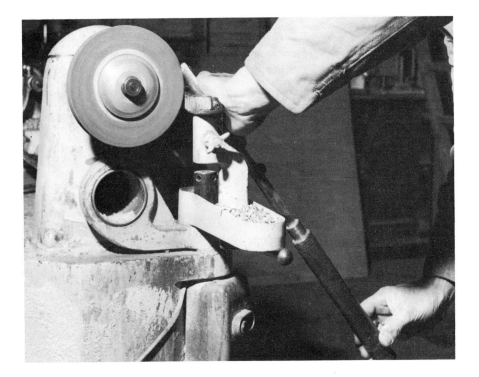

16. Gouge being sharpened on the grindstone. The left hand is used as a pivot and the gouge is rolled from side to side with the fingers and thumb on the handle, the operator standing immediately behind the gouge. The sharpening is started with the bevel heel resting on the stone and *no* pressure is used. (The guard on the grindstone has been removed for the sake of clarity in the photograph.)

pressure on the wheel will burn the edge of the tool in the final stages of sharpening. A star-wheel abrasive dresser is a cheap tool, much more so than a diamond, and a touch or two at long intervals will keep the grindstone in good condition, i.e. a matt, grey dull surface. This tool will also straighten a stone malformed by heavy grinding. Goggles are, of course, essential. I have measured my stone against a new one and have reduced mine to 5″ diameter in some 15 years of work. Carborundum do not make much profit out of me, but at least I admire their product! Grinding accurately with a light touch requires practice and burning gouges is the same as burning money. A good start can be made by endeavouring to grind an even bevel up to say, 1/32″ of the edge and guarding against over-heating by occasionally dipping into cold water. Plunging an extremely hot tool into cold water will eventually damage the metallic structure of the cutting edge, so don't wait too long before cooling. The final honing is given by slipstone and oil. Using a slipstone too often without re-grinding is not to be recommended. It requires great care indeed not to round the bevel after the first couple of honings and this renders the tool hopeless in use. There is another snag that can occur in the first grinding of some new tools. The edge seems to be 'tender' and inclined to go into small gaps as it breaks away from the sparks. I put up with this irregular edge and find that after a few grindings it settles down and more stable steel is reached. I can only think that this 'metal fatigue' is brought on by the factory-ground bevel, but this is only an opinion. Incidentally, the practice of using dry wheels is frowned upon by my own toolmaker, and after seeing the result of some of my students' hamfisted-ness I can only agree with the cautionary notice!

Grinding starts by *resting* the tool perpendicularly against the stone in a position on the tool-rest so that the heel of the bevel is rubbing. It is then rolled slowly from side to side, and as a side comes into view the bright mark of ground steel can be seen. By gently and very slowly lifting the handle this brightness can be seen spreading up the bevel towards the edge. As the tool is resting against the stone, the bevel gradually takes on the curvature of the wheel, producing a hollow ground result. Lifting off the gouge at too frequent intervals is a common cause of uneven grinding, as the tool can seldom be put back into the same 'bed'. The edge takes on the ideal fine burr as the sparks from the stone just reach it. This burr cannot be seen by the holder of the tool, who must compromise by stopping grinding immediately he sees sparks appearing along the top of the tool. A good test that no pressure has been used is when the newly sharpened edge can be immediately grasped by the hand without being too hot to hold. Very little metal is removed when re-sharpening—I am grinding at least three or four times a day and a gouge lasts me a minimum of one year, probably much longer, before it is too short for use.

From my own self-taught experience, I long ago came to the conclusion that knowledge of the correct use of a gouge in bowl turning cannot fully be gained by reading about it or by watching a craftsman demonstrating. It can be compared to learning to ride a bicycle from a book, without a knowledgeable person helping you into the saddle. My youngster tried cycling on his own and broke his arm! He turns quite well with it.

It is just possible that an educational film with slow motion effects, camera aids, soundtracks, etc., would be the answer for teaching a group of students, but as I do not know anyone with a cine-camera, I will try to make do with a ball-point. Consider the following procedures:

(*a*) Cutting from large to small diameter.
(*b*) Starting to cut at 'precise point of entry'.
(*c*) Bevel rubbing on wood.
(*d*) Cutting in an arc.
(*e*) Rolling the gouge.
(*f*) Moving the handle.
(*g*) Stance and footwork.
(*h*) Ambidextrousness.

I can try to explain each requirement, but to use a gouge properly you have to do a combination of some of the above items simultaneously and in unison or you will fall off the bike. It must be easier to write about ballet.

Presentation and Bevel Rubbing

To have the support of the wood helps control the gouge in cutting off the desired thickness of shaving. This seems so obvious to me and is a natural action by an experienced turner who would regard the need to explain it much the same way as a carver would be amazed if someone asked him why he pushed his gouge into his work instead of scraping away the desired quantity of wood.

I ask my students to hold a gouge in a comfortable position and present it to the wood. In every case I find that the gouge is not held with the handle end down enough and the bevel, however short, is therefore nowhere near its proper position. So, in effect, a turner's stance is an unnatural position and he must get accustomed to it. The lathe height could be increased, of course, but this would raise problems in spindle turnery, where sometimes we need the tool to work on the very top of the wood. I present a gouge to a disc almost perpendicularly and held in front of my chest and I am very close to the wood. Most amateurs angle the gouge and follow behind it with pushing action. In a great number of cases they use the horizontal top of the handrest as a guide for the gouge travel, so that in turning the outside of a bowl the gouge is in fact pushed round in an almost horizontal position, the bevel only rubbing occasionally and so much of the wood is taken off by a scraping action. And also, the centre portion of the edge is the only bit used and the 'wings' of the edge remain virginal.

It is rather curious that the metal support is universally called a 'tool-rest', but in Myford's woodturning catalogue it has always been called a 'hand-rest' and this is what it is for. Naturally, the gouge lies on it too, but in a properly controlled cut it can be lying on various parts of the rest and only occasionally is it on the very top edge. The perfect hand-rest has yet to be created and some of them should never have been born. I ground off some of the projecting metal of mine which got in my way, the winged piece directly above the pin, and this portion is now brightly polished by the movement of the tools against it. So it is a hand-rest more than a tool-rest, and it is definitely NOT a tool-guide. The cutting action of the gouge is controlled by the hands, one of them is supported on the hand-rest.

A piece of wood is on the lathe and it is taken that it has been made into a disc by some means, properly or otherwise. 'Chipping' a rough round into a disc is described later, to do it now might confuse. The bevel cannot be laid properly on to irregularly rounded wood and the knocking that results creates nervous tension in beginners, which is to be avoided.

If the wood is free of defects, has no knots or sapwood in awkward places, it is 'proper' to take out the inside of the bowl following the curve of the annual rings. The *end* grain must be looked at to find the direction of these, the roundness of the timber disc can show what may appear to be annual rings in the *side*. Distortion caused by abdominal surgery has already been discussed, annual rings tend to straighten in drying so there is a compensating pull if the wood is turned the proper way. However, if a defect can be removed by not turning it this way, then by all means remove the defect and do not stick slavishly to the rules. My wife, in learning to drive with me as the teacher (and I'm no good at it), came to a 'T' junction at the top of a slight rise and should have turned right. Instead we landed up straight ahead into the hedge. She said that she couldn't turn the wheel and change gear at one and the same time. My gentle rejoinder was to the effect that next time to hell with the gears, just turn the wheel. End of that particular lesson. Back to turning wood.

One method of turning a bowl is to do the outside first, take the half-finished wood off the faceplate, reverse and re-centre it and then remove the inside. This is a waste of time. It is also very difficult indeed to re-centre *exactly*, whatever method is used to try to do so. I think the reason for this practice in some schools is due to the size of the rear-turning faceplate which is supplied as large as a breadboard.

Since nearly everything I can think of can be turned on a faceplate no larger than 6″ diameter, I am at a loss to understand the need for any bigger dimension. In production, my bowls are turned completely on one fixing on the 6″ faceplate, therefore the bases are finished to 6″ diameter. When I need a smaller base I pack out the faceplate with a smaller disc of wood and use screws long enough to go through faceplate, scrapwood, and into the base of the bowl. Then the gouge can go right round without fouling the faceplate. Penetration of screws into the bowl base by ³⁄₈″ is *ample* hold, and four screws long enough to do this will secure a very large bowl indeed. Besides saving time, when a bowl is turned at one fixing, the edge of the bowl can be turned to knife edge thinness if desired, or it can be decorated with beadwork, chamfering, etc. Since turning a bowl in one fixing entails cutting against the grain when the gouge is travelling towards the faceplate, I suppose this is an argument in favour of the first method and I have to mention it because someone is bound to point it out to me. However, my argument is that the bowl must be cut against the grain on two sides anyway, so a little more is permissible in view of the advantages stated. I make it a practice, when demonstrating and lecturing away from home, to ask for a 6″ faceplate to be made available. At the last demonstration I attended the master couldn't find one, so he had just turned down the 'bread-board' to my size! That's what I call initiative, but I don't know what he did about the inventory.

The disc of wood is on the faceplate and the object is to turn it into a bowl. I ask my students to place the gouge on the wood in a position to start rounding the disc towards the faceplate, since a right-hander finds this part easier to do at first. I find that they always position the gouge somewhere in the middle of the outside of the disc. This would mean that in a complete cut the gouge would have to remove a very thick shaving at the faceplate end and this cannot be done. It is much better to start just to the left of the corner of the disc and round this corner off. This is the first stage of turning from large diameter to small, or 'downhill' if you like.

Like gouges I prefer to go downhill myself, possibly because my school was at the top of one. The gouge is placed almost perpendicular and just left of the corner of the wood. The left hand is at the top of the gouge quite near the edge so that the fingers are prevented by the hand-rest from fully encircling the tool. The fleshy part of the hand follows the gouge, the thumb is splayed and the ball resting on the blade. The turner is *behind* the gouge (NOT inclined to the left, so that he can see the left hand bevel).

17a. *Rounding towards the front.* The fleshy part of the *right* hand is behind the gouge and on the hand-rest. The handle is well down and against the *left* leg. The stance and footwork of a turner is completely *opposite* to, say, a carpenter planing wood in the bench vice. The gouge is being rolled to the front in a downward *arc* and shown finishing the cut to 17b.

The bevel should not be seen at all at the start of the cut. The right hand holds the handle well down so that the *heel* of the bevel is touching the wood. The lathe is started, at low speed (a recommended bowl-turning speed is about 700 r.p.m.), and the gouge is rolled round the corner of the disc, with the handle end coming up at the end of the roll. This action is repeated several times and the bevel gradually lowered so that eventually the edge will bite and take off a very light shaving. It will be noted that the

17b. Gouge almost on its side and handle coming up the leg. The cut is completed by twisting or rolling the gouge off the corner.

cutting action of the rolling gouge is in the form of a slight arc from the perpendicular. It will also be noted that the point on the left wing of the gouge edge is taken well clear of the wood by a combination of arc and roll. It is this trailing edge of the gouge that is the culprit behind all the 'digs-in'. The leading edge of the gouge is completely innocent of this wrongdoing.

The rolling of the gouge, the support of the fleshy part of the hand on the rest behind it, and the thumb, prevent the gouge kicking back if it hits a hard streak or knot or suchlike, and inflicting the shock and kind of damage well known to beginners. The arc of the cut keeps the bevel rubbing all the time so that it is supported by timber. Once the corner is rounded the gouge works sweeter and the curve of the bowl can be progressed. The constant roll of the gouge and the lift of the handle end is made really clear if a shaving is started and *kept the same depth* all round the curve of the bowl. The beginner is tense and apprehensive at first, so he unconsciously restricts the movement of the gouge, it therefore 'comes off' halfway round the cut. Taking off a thin shaving of even thickness all round will very soon demonstrate the amount of edge roll and handle movement required. If it can be kept in mind that it is always the corner of the gouge furthest away from the wood and direction of travel that does the 'digging-in', confidence grows by leaps and bounds, and confidence matters a great deal when dealing with a lethal-looking chunk of wood whizzing round at a rate of knots. I call this damage-causing corner of the gouge the 'trailing edge', the other one is the 'leading edge' and will do no damage, in fact I often use this *fully flat* at times inside a bowl.

Another fault of the beginner is that he stands too far away from the work. This might be one way for him to keep the handle down enough for

18a. *Rounding towards the faceplate.*
In previous cuts the corner has been rounded off and the gouge is now shown at the start of another cut. The fleshy part of the *left* hand is behind the gouge and resting on the hand-rest, the fingers are close to the edge of the gouge (better control), and therefore cannot completely encircle the gouge. The thumb helps control the roll of the gouge. The gouge is pointing 'well up', the handle right down and resting against the *right* leg. The cut is completed at—

18b. The gouge is almost completely on its side and the handle has been raised up on the leg. At this stage, the gouge, still rolling, can be pushed forward and down to complete the cut.

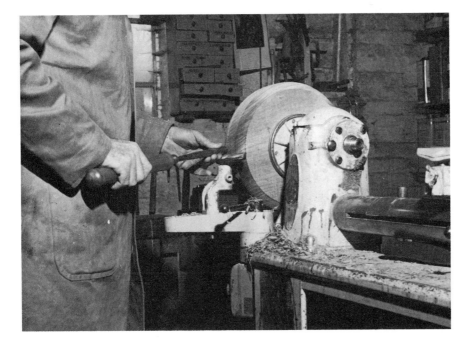

18c. *Completely* wrong.
The gouge is being pushed along the top of the hand-rest, i.e. the rest is being used as a guide. The left hand is pulling the gouge so any tendency to kick back can only be controlled by the tips of the fingers and this is hazardous in the extreme. The handle of the gouge is almost horizontal and completely away from the support of the body. The cut (?) is a scraped one and brute force is needed to keep the gouge in its path. The edge is completely blunted in the first few seconds of the cut. The bevel must rub on the wood to cut it cleanly.
Note. In all these photographs the 'dig-in' point, i.e. the trailing edge of the gouge, is coming *away* from the wood all the time.

the bevel to work, but the best way is to stand close in and bend the knees. This leads me into body movement. Due to the very nature of the revolving wood the gouge is inclined to 'bounce' on the surface and it is a physical effort to try to keep a smooth cut going just using the hands. I am not too fond of physical effort.

The handle of a 'long and strong' is also long, in fact I am not sure if the manufacturers' versions are long enough; my own are at least a foot long and the handle is always resting on some part of my body when I am turning, usually on a leg. Still going from left to right, the handle will be on my right leg, and I can take off a shaving using left hand and right leg alone, because this way my body provides a third 'hand'. With all three controls going, complete mastery of the gouge is achieved whatever the terrain, but to do this, the footwork and stance has to be just right for each cut. It would be wise to ignore all this until the gouge can be used reasonably well without the support of the body, otherwise it could become just another restriction affecting the free movement of the handle.

When the outside of the bowl is rounded satisfactorily to the faceplate end, the curve to the edge is completed with *hands reversed*, the normal way to a left-hander, large diameter to small. Once again the fleshy part of the right hand is behind the gouge. When I tell my right-handed student to do this, he or she is usually aghast at the very thought, but I find that after a few tentative attempts it comes quite naturally and later in the course I only have to say, 'Wrong hands' very occasionally. Using body movements, the gouge now rests on the left leg, otherwise you will look like a contortionist.

Now is the time to instil a little confidence, if you believe all I have written so far. In turning from left to right towards the faceplate, the bevel is in contact with, but not *pressing* on, the timber. The cut is made with the centre and right wing of the blade, and the gouge rolled in this cutting fashion. As long as the tip of the left hand wing does not touch the wood, there is absolutely no danger of a 'dig-in'. You can use as much as you like of the right wing. After the surface has been semi-rounded towards the base, try this experiment. With the bevel in contact, roll the blade all round the surface without cutting. Nothing untoward will happen. So now you do not have to keep your eye glued to the cutting edge. Try some trial runs without looking at the gouge, and without cutting. Now, looking at the gouge, choose some area and start the cut, then look up at the top of the revolving disc for the rest of the cut. This procedure has two distinct benefits. You can see clearly what the cut is doing, and your eyes will tell you what to do to co-ordinate the twisting of the handle and the amount you have to raise it to complete a satisfactory cut. At the same time you can see far more clearly what you are making!

5. Bowl Turning: Inside Work

It is a matter of choice as to where the gouge is entered on the face of the disc to commence removing waste. I have seen some workers who start from the rim and work down towards the centre, leaving a cone in the middle and then taking this down from the other direction. This may be because they are using a 'nosed' gouge and not one ground straight across the top. The point of the nose of the gouge is inclined to get in the way in a deep cut and a clean sweeping cut is difficult to complete.

In rough-turning wet elm, my own practice is to 'countersink' the centre of the disc with the gouge and then, by pushing in, swivelling the gouge to the left and raising up the handle until it is horizontal, I 'push-drill' a deep hole in the centre of the disc, then remove waste from the side of the hole, gradually working back to the rim. Before you even mount the disc on the faceplate, it is of great help to bore, by a drill press, electric drill or even hand-brace, as large a diameter centre hole as you can make. A depth gauge on the drill will allow you to determine the finished thickness of the bowl bottom. The hole need not be at exact centre—the lathe is very tolerant about this.

Wherever one starts to remove waste, there are two points to remember. The most concentration is required at the *point of entry* into the wood. This is where the gouge relies on the user for direction or it can quite easily go the wrong way! The other point is that the nearer the rim the greater the peripheral speed, especially in a large bowl, and the greater risk of the gouge ripping back over the rim and gashing it. Once the gouge has safely entered the wood it creates a groove for itself and the bevel rubbing in this groove will then prevent the gouge from misbehaving, that is, of course, if the point of the trailing edge is kept clear of the wood. This back edge point is the one that can catch in, turn the gouge over and cause a dig-in.

19. *Practising 'precise point of entry'.*

The leading edge can, and should, be used almost to its full extent from the centre to the left hand point. If this point is allowed to touch the wood the only effect is to 'jam' the cut, but it will not do much damage, certainly not to the extent of a dig-in. Fig. 19 shows a method of teaching 'precise point of entry' into the wood. It is left hand turnery again, the fleshy part of the right hand is behind the blade, close to the point and on the hand-rest. The handle is almost horizontal and held against the *left* leg. The dartboard lines have been marked with a pencil while the disc revolves and the exercise is to enter the gouge into the wood on a line and without it slipping back towards the perimeter. The nearer one gets to the outside edge the more difficult the exercise becomes. The gouge is presented *on its side*, the edge gently rubbing on the line, and then pushed below the surface of the wood. Only a little penetration is required and immediately this has been accomplished, the handle is lowered, the blade sent upwards on its arcing cut and at the same time rolled slightly over to the left to keep the trailing point clear of the wood. The arc of the cut is shallow—if it is too pronounced then the gouge will attempt to finish the cut by coming *down* from the top to the centre of the disc, and it is more liable to dig in at this point. A shallow cutting arc will bring the gouge almost horizontal before it reaches the centre and although ending in almost a scrape it is much easier to control.

20. *Start of arcing cut after entry.*

21. *Middle of cut.*

22. *End of cut.*

23. *Use of pointed scraper to limit rim thickness.*

Fig. 20 shows the gouge on its side, almost horizontal and having entered the wood near the rim. Fig. 21 shows the gouge in the middle of its arc, the handle lowered, the left hand leading edge cutting almost to its full width, the gouge being rolled over to the left all the time to keep the trailing point clear of the wood. Fig. 22 shows the gouge at the end of the cut, approaching the centre of the wood from the side (not down from the top). The handle is almost horizontal again and has moved over from the leg to the groin to keep the bevel rubbing as much as possible.

If, in taking a deep controlled width cut, the leading edge is allowed to enter the wood to its full width it will bury itself and jam further progress. It is a mistake to use force to push this through the wood to complete the cut. The correct way is to very slightly roll the gouge over backwards so that the leading edge point comes away from the jam, and then roll forward again to complete the cut with the leading edge point just clearing the wood.

The tension induced by concentrating on 'precise point of entry' is liable to persist, even though the gouge has been entered safely into the wood. This can lead to too much of a 'muscle-cracking' grip on the tool, frustrating its natural cutting action and giving a jerky performance. The remedy is to take not too deep a cut and to try to keep the cut *at the same depth* the whole length of its travel. This makes certain that the gouge is allowed full 'swing' so that it cuts naturally and without effort. When this happens it should then relax the user!

A dig-in of some sort of severity is bound to occur when learning to use a gouge properly. It is also unfortunate that the result of one dig-in is cumulative. At the next endeavour, the gouge finds the dig-in and induces another and another, until the end result is like the product of a drunk ploughing a field. It is probable that the gouge is then thrown across the workshop and the user resorts to the medicine cabinet or the local.

I had a telephone call early one Sunday morning from a sufferer, who in a voice of politely controlled rage requested tuition to be arranged as soon as ever possible or an excellent lathe would be consigned to a Corporation dustcart. George, the patient, is doing quite nicely now. Before this stage is likely to be reached, first aid resort can be made to a scraping tool, the ruts scraped into submission and a new start made with the gouge.

A skew pointed scraper can also be used to determine the limit of the rim edge, Fig. 23. It is held horizontally and the point pushed straight in where desired. It provides a ready made groove for the gouge to enter and it is a good method to use to protect the rim from gouge damage when sufficient practice has not yet been attained.

In bowls of small diameter, the user, standing in the correct position behind the gouge can complete all cuts from rim to centre until the bowl is deep enough. Large diameter bowls are not so amenable, and to attempt to complete the hollowing out in one body-and-legs position may lead to the belief that a turner has to be a born contortionist. The inside of a large bowl is taken out in stages. For instance, when more wood has to be removed to a deeper curve inside, possibly to follow the outside curvature, the turner moves over to the left, his body directly behind the gouge, which is directed at 45 degrees to the rim of the bowl. The gouge is presented on its side, the right hand holding it as a pivot. The handle is held against the body, and waste wood is removed by a scooping action using the movement of the hips alone to swing the gouge. So although turners are not contortionists, they may excel at today's dance routines.

When no further wood can be removed owing to the fact that the waste wood at the bottom is getting in the way, stance is changed and the bottom wood is removed, until the bowl is of relatively even thickness throughout. This even thickness is rather important in doing wet wood turning as too much variation in thickness in parts of the bowl can lead to cracking in the drying out process. In turning seasoned stock this is immaterial.

The 'popular' ⅜" L. & S. gouge can do all the turning that has been described, but the larger gouges have some advantages. They take out more wood at each cut, and in doing fairly deep bowls, where the rest cannot be taken right inside, so that perforce more tool length protrudes without support over the rest, the extra bulk of the large gouge makes it a steadier tool to control, whereas the ⅜" can whip about a little if too much of its blade is over the rest.

Before the roughly finished (and I am not being sarcastic) bowl is taken off the lathe it is helpful, but not essential, if a handful of cheap paste wax (polishing virtues not required) is spread into the bowl, inside and out, while it revolves. A square of cloth holds the wax and as much as possible is forced into the fibres. This treatment seems to prevent a lot of cracks in the drying out stage. A 1" thick rough-turned bowl should be allowed about three months in an airing cupboard temperature (not too hot and with a little humidity) to thoroughly dry out and mis-shape itself to its heart's content, but if there *is* heart in the wood, you are wasting your time as this is bound to create cracks. For the benefit of my transatlantic friends, the 'heart' I refer to is better known to them as 'pith'.

Finish-turning a Roughed-Out Bowl after Seasoning

The extent to which a wet-wood bowl can warp and twist while drying out can be most alarming, but it is very seldom that the distortion is such that a finished circular bowl cannot be obtained from it. The photograph shows a typical example. The timber goes more oval in shape than anything else,

24. The left-hand disc has just been turned from unseasoned elm, and despite the optical illusion from the grain markings, is circular. The centre bowl has dried out and warped considerably in the process. The final product at the right is as the bowl has come off the lathe after a preliminary treatment with sanding sealer.

but of course it twists as well, so the first job is to plane the bottom flat again for the faceplate fixing. Elm, especially English red elm and wych elm, cleans up nicely if it is planed *across* the grain. There is more control and less risk of the grain tearing out. Finishing with abrasive paper wrapped around a cork block, and applied in line with the grain completes the job. When the disc was first rough-turned, two of the screw holes for the faceplate should have been positioned in line with centre and grain, and now the wood has dried out, these two holes will not have altered their position much, and the faceplate can be refixed in its original place. The other two holes may have 'travelled' considerably! It should be perfectly safe to finish the bowl secured by two holes alone, but if the turner is of a pessimistic nature, the other two can be used, the screws going in 'skew' to find them and not driven too far home so that the heads bite into and possibly damage the faceplate. Sufficient wood will have been removed when planing flat, to ensure that the short screws have sufficient grip.

The bowl is put on the lathe and the rest positioned so that the outside can be turned first. Since the wood is not round, care is needed to ensure that the rest is close to, but does not foul the wood, and this is tested by revolving by hand before switching on the motor.

Some amateurs get quite worried about the precise height of the hand-rest, and this is not really important, as long as the tool being used with it is not cutting below centre height. My own hand-rest is always down on the toolpost as far as it will go and I have got used to it at this level. It saves me the slight fiddling job of always adjusting it.

With most bowls of reasonably large sizes, say over 6″ diameter, the lathe should be run at a low speed, about 700 r.p.m. Higher speeds increase vibration, do not allow the tool time to cut well, and soon blunt an edge.

25. The bottom of a dried-out rough-turned bowl in the process of being planed flat to receive the faceplate in readiness for final turning.

26. Using the edge of the plane to test the flatness of the base. Note that it is being planed across the grain.

27. A disc, roughly rounded by bandsawing, being brought down to a true circle with the gouge. The bevel at the correct angle for rubbing on the wood where possible. Gouge being pushed from right to left, right hand close to edge of tool and long handle held against the body for control and steadying.

Even when turning a dry roughed-out bowl at lowest speed some vibration is bound to occur until the outside of the bowl is turned absolutely circular again. This is accomplished by the same method as used when rounding a roughly-bandsawn disc. The gouge, preferably a stout ½″ long and strong is held with the handle well down (almost perpendicular), in such a position that the bevel would rub if it could. Looking at the top of the revolving bowl will reveal a distinct shadow of waste wood which has to be cut away before the wood is truly circular. This can be a good guide. Fluorescent lighting directly over the lathe is not recommended as this tends to dispel these useful shadows. The centre top of the gouge is brought down until the cutting edge starts to take off small chips of wood, and the disc is then traversed at this same angle without any rolling action of the gouge. If care is taken to remove the shadow in even stages there is less risk of a dig-in, and soon the bevel will be rubbing on a larger area of wood and then the normal action of the gouge can be used, and the bowl brought down to the finished shape.

When practice has at least given the amateur some understanding of gouge control and correct cutting action, there still remains the big problem of end-grain, i.e. the two areas of a disc where the tool has perforce to cut against the grain and therefore will disturb it to a degree, depending upon good gougework, type of wood, or both. A sharp gouge and light cuts will keep the roughness down to a minimum, so obviously this is recommended, but it is seldom completely successful in taming the roughness. Anyone who has had to plane a cross-grained board in benchwork has the same difficulty however sharp the smoothing plane. He can help it with a close-set cap-iron, or a block plane designed for the purpose and used diagonally across the grain. The turner has a similar aid. This is a deep fluted, long and strong ¼″ bowl-turning gouge, ground straight across or with just a suggestion of a point. Bevelled the same as the larger gouges, it can be used straight from the grindstone, but if one is 'ham-fisted' at this operation, the gouge can be finish-sharpened with oil and slipstone.

Backing Up

In explaining the correct action of a bowl turning gouge, great stress has been made on rolling the gouge so that the trailing point is continually coming away from the wood, since it is this point that is mainly responsible for digs-in. However, in the operation of cleaning up end grain with the ¼″ gouge, the closer this dangerous point can be brought to the revolving wood the better the result! Of course if it happens to touch the wood then damage is bound to occur. The beginner can proceed by stages and will improve as experience (and courage!) increases. The cut is started in the normal way and we will assume that the cleaning up operation has been started on the outside of the bowl, from the middle to the rim, i.e. from right to left. Note that it is not possible to do this 'backing-up' on the *inside* of the bowl. Also that cutting on the outside of a bowl is always done from the largest diameter to the smallest, e.g. from the middle 'bulge' to the narrower rim, and again from the middle 'bulge' to the smaller base. In normal cutting, from right to left the larger gouges would be rolled the same way. In backing-up with the ¼″ gouge, once the cut has been started, the edge is *backed against* the wood, with the handle coming up at the same time so that the cut is a downward slicing arc across the grain fibres. The beginner can be cautious in backing the gouge only slightly at first, so that the *whole* of the right hand edge is not on the wood. He will only be able to accomplish a very short distance (possibly ½″) before the gouge, of its own accord, comes away from the incomplete cut. However, he will have managed a sliced cut, despite its short duration, and can start again where the gouge left off, completing the outside of the bowl in a succession of slight ridges. These should be slight, because in backing-up only very fine

28a. Backing up with ¼″ long and strong deep fluted gouge. Start of a slicing cut from right to left. The centre and left-hand edge of the gouge has just started a light cut at a high angle (top of arc).

28b. The slicing cut being continued, the gouge centre still in the cutting path, but the edge brought back so that nearly all the right-hand edge is doing the cutting.

28c. Progressing down the slight arc, note difference in angle from back edge cutting but 'dig-in' point not touching the wood.

28d. The finish of the backing-up cut, which helps to smooth down the end-grain.

cuts are needed. These backing-up slicing cuts of the small gouge do wonders for the disturbed fibres of end grain and cut them cleanly. The rest of the bowl benefits too, but it should not really need it, and only gets it because it is going around with the rest of the wood! The easiest part of the outside of the bowl is from centre to rim where the curvature is usually not too pronounced. Backing-up in the other direction, i.e. around the bowl to the faceplate is correspondingly difficult. However, once this backing-up has been tried and a successful 'strip' of cut obtained, the beginner will be persuaded to practise it until, with increasing confidence, he can bring the 'wrong' side of the gouge on to the wood for almost its full width and complete the backing-up process all round the bowl in a possible maximum of four slices.

Scraping

When the outside of the bowl has been completed to the desired shape, using only gougework, then it is ready for the surface to be improved by the use of scraping tools. Improper use of these tools is by far the main reason for poorly finished turnery work. A sharp gouge, chisel, or even a plane blade will remove wood when applied at a scraping angle, i.e. where the bevels are not touching the wood, and the first few cuts can be effective. The trouble is that the keenest edge, applied in this way, lasts only seconds before it is blunted, and as soon as the edge is lost then damage to the fibres of the wood inevitably follows. End grain suffers the most, because it is raked up the 'wrong' way and in severe cases small tufts of wood are actually torn out. No amount of abrasive paper will heal this damage. The correct use of scrapers follows the same pattern and sequence used by a cabinet-maker, who would never dream of starting on sawn wood immediately with a cabinet scraper or scraper plane. He may first bring it down with a jackplane (our ½″ gouge), following up with a smoothing plane (⅜″ gouge), and perhaps cleaning up with a finely set iron or block plane (backing-up ¼″ gouge). Only when all this has been done to the best of his tool-work and ability does he finish with a scraper to *improve* the already good surface he has now obtained, and he would never use a scraper to remove anything like large quantities of wood.

All kinds of tool steel are brought into use as turnery scrapers, from old car springs, mortice chisels, sawblades, file steel, and high-speed steel bars. This is not good practice. Big, *thick* old files make good tools for this purpose, but the emphasis is on thickness and strength, and I am uncomfortably aware of their brittle nature, despite their bulk. A snapping file can behave like a shrapnel bomb.

29. An old *thick* file ground for use as a scraper. Top edge bevelled down to remove serrations and reach softer steel, angle of cutting bevel blunt rather than acute.

Softening them may remove this danger, but can reduce their effectiveness as scrapers. With an old file, it is necessary, although somewhat tedious if taken carefully to avoid burning and ruining the steel, to remove the serrations by grinding them off for some inches from the edge of the tool. It has then to be ground off towards the centre to get to 'softer' steel, and finally ground to the desired cutting shape. Grinding down to a slight angle to the edge so that the best scraping steel (middle of the file thickness) is reached will, of course, reduce the thickness of the cutting edge, so that a thin file is made thinner, and therefore more dangerous. It is bad practice to make the cutting bevel too acute. A blunt angle is stronger and supports the cutting burr better, and since the tool should be used pointing slightly down, i.e. handle up, a blunt bevel is never in the way. Some perfectionists claim that the scraper has to be held exactly horizontal to the floor. This, academically, is correct, but could be difficult to maintain in an even sweep over the surface, because even the slightest drop of the handle below horizontal can lead to 'dig-in' problems.

A famous Sheffield firm now manufactures scrapers to my specifications. They are of high-speed steel throughout so that they need not be reduced in thickness, have no serrations to remove, are wide and heavy and each of the set of six is already ground to a basic shape most used in turnery. The blunt bevels are also factory-ground. This firm was very helpful and patient in meeting my rather exacting demands on their skill and knowledge of steel.

There is, of course, no question of the 'bevel rubbing' when applying a scraper. The bevel is always away from the work, and it is important that the cutting edge is always trailing slightly on the wood. Pointing the scraper upwards into the wood is asking for trouble, as it would easily dig in, causing unnecessary damage to the bowl, and to the nerves. With good clean gougework very little wood need be further removed by the scraper, but although applied lightly against the wood, some pressure is needed on the tool. This is in a downward thrust on the hand-rest. If the scraper was allowed to have its own way it would 'bounce' on the hard and soft grain as

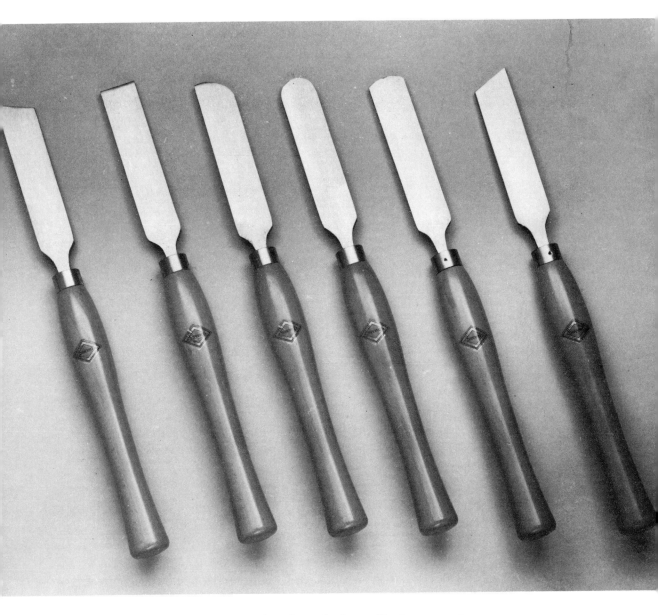

30. Set of six scrapers made in high-speed steel to author's specification concerning shape and strength. (Henry Taylor Tools, Sheffield. Brand name: Diamic.)

the bowl revolved against it, defeating the object of a smooth finish. If, however, the scraper is heavy, has a good long stout handle, this can be tucked into the body as extra support, and, together with downward pressure on the hand-rest, can be controlled with ease, operating without judder. It seems so logical that the more delicate the work, the smaller and finer the tool used, but this is not so in turnery. The 'weightier' the scraper,

31. Heavy scraping tool in use. Handle held against body for steadying to reduce vibration.

the finer the finish. Although the scraper 'burr' cannot technically be described as a cutting edge, when used properly it will bring off small curled shavings. When it only brings off dust it just isn't sharp enough.

Sharpening is fairly easy. First, the top of the scraper is cleaned to remove any traces of old burr. This can be done with a flat carborundum stone. Then the heel of the bevel is placed on the front of the grindstone and the handle gradually lifted until sparks just appear at one corner of the top of the scraper. This angle is held and the scraper taken across the grindstone so that the sparks travel all the way along the cutting edge. In a straight or skew scraper this would be accomplished by taking the scraper straight across the stone, in a curved scraper it would have to be rotated as well. With the grindstone accessory on the Myford lathe, the small turning hand-rest can be brought up close to the front and used as a grinding support for the scraper. The top edge of the rest is narrow, which allows easy manoeuverability of the scraper when sharpening. The snag about using a self-standing grinder, single or double ended, is that they are usually equipped with a grinding 'table' and this makes free-hand grinding rather more difficult.

The edge brought up from the grinding wheel can be improved by honing on a carborundum stone and oil, or ticketing in the fashion of

32. Sharpening a heavy scraper. Heel of bevel at one corner brought to bear on grindstone, sparks directed downward. The scraper is slowly lifted until the sparks appear on top of the edge of the tool and the whole edge taken across at this angle to complete the sharpening. Note dark patch at side of arbor where the grindstone dresser has not been able to reach. (The guard on the grindstone has been removed for the sake of clarity in the photograph.)

cabinet makers with their handscrapers. Personally I never use up time in doing this. The edge direct from the stone does not last long on the wood being scraped, but re-sharpening on the grindstone is so quickly done, and so little metal is removed by doing so, that I find this method much more convenient. I get very little pleasure out of sharpening tools, I am only too anxious to get them back to the job.

When it has been decided that the surface cannot be further improved by more scraping with the heavy tools, the process can be repeated using a bar of high-speed steel. Large planer blades salvaged from the big machines used by timber merchants are ideal for the job, but alas very scarce. I buy high-speed steel bars about a foot long, 1½″ wide and at least ⅛″ thick. It is expensive material. The short edge is blunt-bevelled and sharpened on the grindstone in the same way as the 'heavies', and gentle handling here gives a really beautiful fine burr which will bite viciously into the wood if allowed to. It is applied to the revolving disc in the same way as the heavy scraper, but much more lightly and can do much in the way of

33. Close-up of scraper action. Bevel away from wood, tool being pointed down to trail. Burr edge removes small shavings, when blunted will only remove dust.

improving the surface. Then it can be used in what may appear to be a dangerous fashion, but this is not in fact so. The hand-rest and anything else likely to get in the way is removed, the high-speed blade held firmly near the edge, pointed downward below the centre of the disc, and, using the wood itself as a support, gently scraped. The absence of the hand-rest allows much more movement and the risk of damage is negligible, since any 'snag' will only result in the scraper coming safely away from the wood. This 'free-hand' scraping must not on any account take place *inside* a bowl.

When all this has been accomplished, the revolving surface of the outside of the bowl should feel silken smooth with perhaps a trace of roughness at the two 'difficult' areas.

Even so, the perfectionist will not be so easily satisfied and we have yet another process for him to try. When a pupil has accomplished all the foregoing, and is lightly feeling the revolving wood with the tips of his fingers and smiling with satisfaction, I stop the lathe. A little sleight of hand at the motor, the lathe is started once more and I ask the pupil to 'feel again'. The

34. Using a high-speed scraping bar 'by hand', with the lathe going in reverse. Edge pointing downwards and below centre of bowl.

smile is instantly removed, because where before had been a silken flow of wood is now a distinct roughness. The motor has in fact been reversed and the bowl is revolving in the opposite direction to its normal travel. This shows that the action of a scraper, however sharp and gentle in application, lays down the wood fibres in one direction. The man who uses a blade razor knows this well. A 'scrape' down his cheek and it feels smooth in that direction, but his fingers rubbing upwards reveal an enormous difference.

With the bowl now going round the opposite way, I move to the other side of the lathe and 'free-hand scrape' the surface with the high-speed steel bar. There is, of course, no hand-rest. The pupil, staying where he is, follows the path of my scraper with his fingers, and the smile on his face comes back again as the smoothness 'miraculously' reappears.

Reversing an electric motor is a simple matter with the incorporation of a change-over switch, as discussed in chapter three. There is however one important aspect to consider. With the disc going in the opposite direction, the screw-thread holding the faceplate is going the 'wrong' way, thus the possibility arises of its unwinding itself off the headstock. There is no question of the wood and faceplate coming off violently and hurling itself through the air. It will unscrew, stop for an instant in time, and then drop down to the floor, usually on to your unwary foot.

One quite reliable way of prevention is to put a hand-made solid leather washer, about $\frac{1}{8}''$ thick on to the headstock spindle and make sure that this is always squeezed tight by the faceplate when screwing this on. The friction of the leather will allow quite heavy 'opposite' work to be done before it releases the faceplate. The pessimist can drill and tap a hole in the faceplate spindle and use a grubscrew to fasten the faceplate securely to the headstock spindle. Whatever method is used, I find the ability to reverse my lathe at will very handy for all sorts of odd jobs.

To sum up to now, the wet wood disc has been rough-turned, seasoned, base planed flat again and rechucked, and the outside only has been cut to finished shape, and scraped with heavy and light scrapers, with additional light scraping in reverse. The outside surface is now ready for cleaning up with abrasive paper. In turning a seasoned disc, the same procedure applies, the outside finished first before any hollowing out is attempted.

Getting a perfect finish from scraping tools is not, as usually implied, easy to do. I now have the task of reading and reviewing many newly published works on the craft, especially from overseas, where interest in woodturning is steadily rising. The photographs are usually very clear and of excellent quality. So much so that the appalling finish is readily discernible to the practised eye, and I regret that this seems to be accepted by some authors as normal.

To understand more fully, the reader can try an experiment. First, complete a small area to a really good gouge-cut finish. Try by this method to gain an almost polished surface from the cutting tool alone. Now choose half this area and use a scraper. Even on a very good surface, the scraper tends to bounce a little back and forth. If the tool is held as firmly as it should be, this sensation can be felt by the turner. Now each forward bounce can disturb and even pull out fibres on the end grain areas. By using the scraper with excessive pressure against the wood, this cancels out the bounce, but the result is deplorable as you will probably find out when you stop the lathe and compare the scraped, 'finished' surface with the untouched cut area. Playing a light over the surface at various angles will help to pick out the difference. Prepare a new cut surface and try again. Imagine that the surface that is to be improved by the scraper is not an even one at all. It is made up of many small hills and hollows. You use the scraper to remove the hilltops but *not* the hollows. When you can achieve a finish which is as good, or better, than your cut surface, then the practice will have paid off.

6. Bowl Turning: Finish-turning and Polishing

The rim of the bowl should be faced as the first operation, since to try to insert a gouge into an uneven front just makes things that much more difficult. A ⅜" gouge is the handiest cutting tool for the facing job. The rest is placed directly in front and across the edge, and as near to it as the wobbling rim will allow. The gouge is held, bevel 'well up', handle down, almost vertical, and in such a position that it can be rolled across the rim from the outside in, cutting chips as it rolls across the uneven surface. Light cuts of course, and the rim tested frequently with the tips of the fingers which will soon convey by touch alone that all irregularities have been removed and the rim is completely even.

The next job is to reduce the rim to the required finished thickness. This operation causes most beginners a great deal of trouble until they learn to be master of the gouge and not the other way round. As soon as they touch the wood with the tool it rips back in the wrong direction and gashes the edge. Their next attempt, and the gouge finds the runaway track made the first time and off it goes again, increasing the damage. The correct way is to present the gouge on its side (hollow towards the centre of the bowl), in an almost horizontal position, with the centre of the edge, where the point would be if there was a point, just touching and rubbing the wood at the required point of entry. The gouge is held very firmly indeed and slowly pushed into the wood. As soon as it is safely entered then the danger of ripping back is past, since the cutting edge is now under the surface of the wood and the wood rim is acting as a fence to stop the gouge from misbehaving sideways.

This procedure of making the gouge cut exactly where required (most important when sizing the thickness of the bowl rim), can be called 'precise point of entry'—a term I have used before. Until experience has given confidence, the sharp point of a scraper can be used initially to provide a channel and a fence for the gouge to work in and keep it to its path.

As much cutting as possible is done with the gouge to finish the inside of the bowl. Leaving a lot for a curved scraper to remove is bound to lead to disappointment in the finish, especially where end grain is concerned. It takes up too much time, too! Then the inside, from the rim to somewhere near the centre, is tackled with the curved scraper—a heavy cut is never taken, and the scraper frequently sharpened. When satisfied, the rest is moved inside and across the face, and a domed scraper used from the centre pip outwards to meet the finished side. For safety and also for clean cutting, it must not be forgotten that scrapers are used with the edge pointing slightly downwards, i.e. in a trailing position. Pointing a scraper upwards into wood can be highly hazardous, especially using old files. The domed scraper does a fairly satisfactory job of levelling the bottom of the inside, but in a large bowl some area of the bottom looks best when it is perfectly flat, and this is most difficult to achieve with a rounded scraper. It can leave the bowl with the vestige of a dimple at the centre or a raised peak, neither of which enhances the finished appearance. A scraper ground straight across is the best way to ensure a perfectly flat bottom and the method of using this will be discussed later when table tops and other flat surfaces are dealt with.

Sanding and Stopping

It is essential that the wood is ready in all respects for final finish-polish. No finish can improve a bad surface, and in some cases it will only enhance and draw attention to the faults. Finishing turnery starts with the first revolution of the lathe. Abrasive papers are good finishing tools but before these are used, the wood should be cut, and in the case of bowls, finish-scraped to a smooth, blemish-free surface. Using a coarse grade is no solution as this in itself can damage the fibres beyond repair. A puzzled reader wanted to know, 'Why do cracks appear, across the grain, on otherwise successfully(?) completed work at the final sanding and polishing stage?' The answer is obvious. Too much sanding, perhaps in an attempt to get rid of faults which should not have been there in the first place, creates heat on the surface and then it dries out too quickly, causing very fine cracks to appear.

Small natural faults in the wood such as minor cracks, knot holes etc., can be invisibly mended by the application of wood stopper. This is not to be confused with wood grain filler—quite a different material. Stopper can be obtained in a wide range of wood colours and can be mixed to get the

35a. *Finishing the inside of a rough-turned bowl.*
Using a heavy rounded scraper to finish from edge to bottom area. Limit of swing shown by pencil line. Note left hand acting as pivot and scraper pointing downward. This area can be lightly scraped in both directions, from rim to line and back again, the scraper being slowly 'fed-in' to produce a smooth flowing inside curve without any ridging.

exact shade required. The final colour should be slightly darker than the surround, as when the paste hardens it tends to lighten the shade just a trifle. If the mixture gets too hard to spread, it can be softened with water. Brummer, the brand I use, does not shrink, but I still apply it liberally, and when hard hand-sand away the surplus until all excess or spread-over is removed and only the fault covered. This is essential, as the slightest trace where not needed will eventually show up in the finished surface. When filling an open knot, an incomplete mix of a light and dark colour will resemble a real knot flush with the surface. Lathe sanding can then follow, and finally, hand sanding the interior bottoms of platters and bowls in line with the grain. This helps to remove the fine circular scratches that lathe sanding produces.

35b. *Finishing the inside of a rough-turned bowl.*
The inside curve has been finished first. The domed heavy scraper is now being used
from centre outwards to join the inside curve at the pencil line. Hand-rest well inside
bowl and straight across. Scraper pointing downwards, light scraping action only.
Final flattening of bottom area will be finished with heavy straight across scraper
(method described in chapter eight).

Four grades of opencoat paper (I prefer garnet to any other) are ample.
The commonly available cabinet paper as used by carpenters, cabinet
makers etc., is close-coated and has too stiff a backing to get fully into
turned surfaces. I use a German brand of finishing paper. For all turnery I
use 100 grit followed up by 150 grit. In bowl work these are sufficient for
almost all woods, but some fine-grained fruitwoods sometimes benefit by
the application of 220 grit. All my lathes are fitted with reversing switches
so that the item can be sanded from both directions, an essential for a good
finish (see chapter three) A leather washer is needed to prevent the
faceplate unscrewing itself, as described on page 24.

As a rough guide to how much sanding is required let us take a salad
bowl made from a disc 12″ × 12″ × 3″ thick. An 11″ × 9″ sheet of 100 grit

is folded in half three times, finishing up as a small manageable and flexible pad. The inside of the bowl is sanded first. Rotating from left to right the lower right-hand quadrant of the interior is the safest place to hold the pad. It is held in the left hand with the elbow pressed tightly into the body to provide control and maximum pressure. Without exception, all my pupils attempt sanding with their thumbs *underneath* the paper. More surface contact can be obtained by just using four fingers with the thumb away from the paper. This just takes a little practice, and if at first the paper escapes the hold, it is advisable to let it fly into limbo and recover it from wherever it lands. The pad must be kept moving so that heat is not generated at any one point sufficient to inflict small cracks. Even with the help of the elbow held hard to the body, the exact centre can give trouble, but gripping the wrist with your free hand will overcome this. When half of the sheet is used, the rotation is reversed for the other half. The paper wears most in the centre area, leaving usable areas in the corners, all of which can be applied to the bowl exterior by standing in front and using both hands (no thumbs), to keep the paper moving on the top of the bowl. A doctor pupil told me that wood cellulose, unlike others, cannot be digested by the body, so a light mask is recommended. The whole procedure is repeated with 150 grit, and then if there are rough areas remaining, more toolwork practice is definitely needed!

Sealing and Polishing

The next step is to remove the bowl from the lathe, and with the aid of a cloth pad rub in a generous quantity of cellulose *sanding* sealer. There are a number of sealers on the market, but the essential word to look for is 'sanding'. All my turnery, with the possible exception of stained work, gets this treatment. It acts as a slight grain filler, but its main purpose is to provide a full base or ground for any other polish, wax, varnish, paint, oil, or whatever you have in mind. Sanding sealer will accept a top coat of almost anything, and give it a great deal more depth of finish than can be provided by the top coat alone. It is composed of clear cellulose lacquer and an industrial lubricant—stearate. When the coating is hard dry, the stearate content enables it to be sanded velvet smooth without any clogging of the sanding paper. Excess sealer comes away in a cloud of white dust, so if too much has been applied it is easily dealt with. If too little, then the base is not nearly as well prepared, and even a generous coat of the additional finish-polish will leave the whole looking starved and of little depth.

For bowl turning it is recommended that the sealer is left for twelve hours or overnight to harden fully. Between-centre work can be accelerated by applying a handful of shavings. Cellulose sanding sealer is not recommended for stained work as some stains can react adversely to it. When I stain, and I do so rarely, I use an alternative, a shellac-based sanding sealer.

When hard dry the bowl is returned to the lathe and lightly sanded with worn 150 grit, followed by vigorous use of 000 wire wool. A coarser grade of wool can leave fragments which can eventually discolour and spoil the finish. 0000 grade is expensive, and not necessary.

If tool and scraping work is satisfactory, a good sanding sealer finish looks better than many commercial items offered for sale, and we have only just started! There are three polishes that can be fully completed by lathe alone—wax, oil, and friction polish.

Lathe Wax

A mixture of beeswax and turpentine is a very old recipe for polish, but it is not too successful in turnery. Any end grain in the work absorbs more than the rest of the surface, and the finish can be patchy and sometimes sticky. The hardest natural wax is carnauba from Brazil, and the best choice for us is first grade yellow lumps. Some say apply direct to the spinning wood, but I don't agree. It is almost brick-hard and can inflict scratches. It has a high melting point, and therefore insufficient friction can leave rings of unmelted wax. There is no binding agent in it, so the finish is *on* the wood—not in it, and can flake off. A mixture that I have used for years, and make for commercial resale, is a combination of carnauba, beeswax, and turpentine. Genuine turpentine—there is no alternative. For turnery, the mix is one part by weight carnauba, three to four parts beeswax, and a generous addition of turpentine. I use a double skin boiler, the outer skin containing boiling water which has to be kept topped up. Any plastic food container (such as a yoghurt pot) will accept the fully melted mixture, which solidifies fairly quickly. Since our friendly bee does not always produce the identical product each time, I use a petro-chemical substitute in the mixture that I sell so as to maintain standard quality.

Fortunate turners with supplies of beeswax to hand need only to purchase the carnauba and turpentine. Increasing the amount of beeswax makes the final product a softer and softer mix, until, with the addition of a tin of appropriately tinted shoe polish, a mixture can be obtained to delight the lady of the house for her furniture—far cheaper and better than can be bought. The mix for turnery is exceptionally economical—only a very thin layer is required, applied when the lathe is in motion, then burnished by friction and a soft cloth. One ¼lb block will easily do fifty to sixty large fruit bowls, but don't forget the prior use of sealer.

Finishing oil

Sold under various trade names including Teak Oil, Danish Oil, Swedish Oil, etc, these mostly contain linseed oils, and terebene which is a chemical drier. The oils, which are intended for joinery and cabinet work, are in most cases too thick for the woodturner, and require time to harden.

The ideal oil for us has to be very thin (low viscosity), so that it can be hardened and finished just by friction, with no waiting time. For bowl work, spread a thin coat inside and outside with the lathe at rest, then start the machine and burnish inside and out at the same time, using two cloths and both hands. In a very short time the finish is hard and not in the least sticky. The bowl should be almost hot to touch with the friction exerted. The initial gloss look soon fades to matt. Ideal for salad bowls, supposedly waterproof, but better described as 'wipe with a damp cloth'. My American friends speak highly of tung oil, a pale yellow pungent drying oil from Chinese tung trees, used chiefly in quick-drying varnishes and paints as a waterproofing agent. Sounds fine, but apparently it is expensive. Some trade name oils contain small quantities.

Lathe Friction Polish

Ordinary French polish can be used, but great care is needed to make sure the polishing mop does not catch and grab, ruining the finish.

A friction polish is high grade white French polish containing a solvent which in small diameter turnery never drags, and quickly produces a genuine French polish. The secret in application is to use as little as possible to cover the greatest area. For example take a small table lamp base, with a column of up to 3″ diameter, which has been treated with sander sealer, dried with friction, then lightly sanded with 320 grit. You take a small pad of surgical cotton or batting, put it over the open top of the bottle of polish, and then tip the bottle up and quickly back again to upright. This tiny amount of polish is applied sparingly with the lathe stopped, and turned slowly by hand to give an even all-over coat. Any surplus polish remaining on the pad is pressed away against the back of your hand. The lathe is then started, and the base burnished, lightly at first, then with ever-increasing pressure. A beautiful hard gloss is obtained very quickly indeed. To ensure success, the polishing mop should be as dry as it was before the polish was applied to it.

The finish can be handled right away but does not harden completely for twelve hours, so a good final tip is to spread a thin top coat of turnery wax and burnish it with the same polishing mop. This gives good protection and also complements the finish. Friction polish can be used on larger diameters but the solvent becomes less and less efficient, and fine rings of polish will appear. These, when hard, can be sanded lightly away, and the final polish is done by hand with the lathe stopped.

A warning about leaving polish mops and rags lying around—they have been known to cause spontaneous combustion, so should be destroyed as soon as used.

Polyurethane

When I was in trade, turning out large quotas of bowls, I used to spray a batch at a time with a matt polyurethane finish. This was invisible, and gave a finish that was velvety smooth to the touch. Then I became a victim of severe bilious attacks, but had the luck to have a chemist pupil (I get all sorts!), and he told me that the human body will tolerate the substance until build-up, at which stage it becomes poisonous for some users. If you do not object to the faintly yellowing effect on the timber, polyurethane can be used, but with full breathing protection.

Rustins Clear Plastic Gloss Finish

Not really meant for turnery use, but this is a very fine polish indeed. For the technically minded it is a butylated urea-formaldehyde mixture containing melamins and alkyd. Quite a mouthful. It comes in a pack of four containers, the liquid itself, a hardening catalyst, burnishing cream, and a brush cleaner solvent. When prepared for use it is a water-clear mix which will last twelve hours before it is unusable. The bowl is given a varnish brush flow-coat and left to harden for a period of one hour, but not two hours. In between these times, the bowl is lightly sanded on the lathe to get rid of nibs etc., and a second coat applied. The comprehensive instructions supplied with the kit state that still more coats can be given but I have never met a wood that requires them. The polishing or burnishing cream is made for hand use, so if applied on the lathe neat it will remove all finish in ten seconds flat! The answer is to use a water soaked pad together with the cream, and work up a slurry with the lathe at lowest speed, stopping every fifteen seconds to clean off the mess and inspect the work. The final finish can be worked up to polished glass, or to any stage before. Be warned that nothing will dissolve the finish once it is hard, hence the special brush cleaner. The final finish will withstand dropping on the floor, any alcohol or spirit, eating or drinking vessels can be washed in an automatic dishwasher, and it is unaffected by cleaner or boiling water. There is a similar kit which provides the finest blue-black ebonised colour I have ever seen.

Wood-to-Wood Finish

Effective for very hard woods and therefore extremely useful in ornamental turnery work where even a liquid finish can tend to blur the very fine and crisp detail. Shavings of the same wood are applied at speed, and a lasting polish can be obtained by this method alone. Sometimes small pieces of the same wood are used as burnishing sticks. Similar techniques apply to ivory and bone turnings. Using this method on 'soft' hardwoods will only result in a very temporary polish.

Treatment of Bowl Bases (left with screw holes)

Fruit bowls look well finished with a baize bottom. Old billiards cloth (clean one side) can be used, and hot Scotch glue is an ideal adhesive. Fablon now make a self-adhesive baize, and this can be used instead. Cutting a circle out with scissors is difficult to do neatly. A plywood template turned to the size of the base, plus a keen marking knife, makes a far better job. The paper backing of the self-adhesive baize is pulled off and the cloth applied, sticking instantly and securely. The newest material is green vinyl, which has the advantage of being waterproof and cuts cleanly.

Salad bowls should be washable, or at least made to clean with a damp cloth, so a cloth bottom is unsuitable. The screwholes can be filled, as described, with wood stopping, which when dry is sanded off clean and level. Another method is to obtain a leather worker's tool called a wad punch, ½″ diameter, and with this cut out small discs, or buttons, of thin leather. Scraps of suitable leather can be obtained for next to nothing from a saddler or leather goods maker. The discs are glued over the screw holes, forming small 'feet', and most glues are suitable.

A popular method of making bowls that have no trace of screwholes is to turn the base first with a suitable plinth base. This is then fitted, jammed or lightly glued to a scrapwood disc already on the faceplate, and then the bowl hollowed out and finished. We now have an excellent metal chuck which does this much more easily and safely, and is accurate (see later).

7. Turning Wooden Bowls with High-Speed Steel Tools

The advent of high-speed steel tools has brought with it a number of new approaches to woodturning. This article by my son Roy, first published in *Woodworker* magazine, is included here to consider certain aspects of bowl turning with the use, and ideal design, of these tools particularly in mind.

Turning wooden bowls can be a satisfying pastime, though many would-be bowl turners are frustrated and discouraged by rough patches on the end grain which seem extremely tedious to remove. I believe the problem is partly due to incorrect technique with the bowl gouge and partly due to the poor design of most gouges available these days.

The rough patches occur typically at two places on the outside of the bowl (Fig 36a). They also occur at points on the inside. At these points the fibres of the wood stick out in a direction such that the edge of the tool lifts out the grain and separates the fibres to cause 'sore patches'. The damage can go very deep into the surface depending on the tool used. A heavy cut with a partially blunt scraper can inflict serious injury causing the fibres to separate to a depth of ¼".

Even a good sharp gouge taking a fine cut in the conventional way with the bevel rubbing usually produces deep sore patches. It is impractical to sand or scrape away the damage down to the undisturbed fibres because so much wood has to be removed.

The rough patches can be lightly sanded smooth and can look satisfactory before a finish is applied. But because the areas of disturbed wood fibres are more absorbent than the surrounding material they go a shade darker when polished and can look ugly.

Heavy sanding causes other problems. It is expensive on paper and tedious. The heat of sanding causes the surface of the wood to dry out and

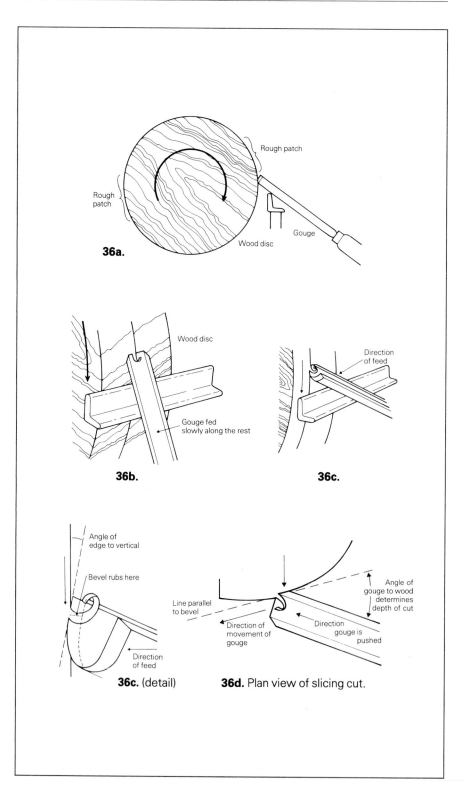

36a.

Rough patch

Rough patch

Wood disc

Gouge

36b.

Wood disc

Gouge fed
slowly along the rest

36c.

Direction
of feed

36c. (detail)

Angle of
edge to vertical

Bevel rubs here

Direction
of feed

36d. Plan view of slicing cut.

Line parallel
to bevel

Direction of
movement of
gouge

Direction
gouge is
pushed

Angle of
gouge to wood
determines
depth of cut

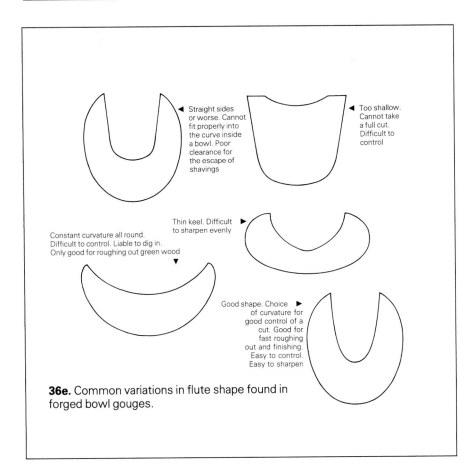

Straight sides or worse. Cannot fit properly into the curve inside a bowl. Poor clearance for the escape of shavings

Too shallow. Cannot take a full cut. Difficult to control

Thin keel. Difficult to sharpen evenly

Constant curvature all round. Difficult to control. Liable to dig in. Only good for roughing out green wood

Good shape. Choice of curvature for good control of a cut. Good for fast roughing out and finishing. Easy to control. Easy to sharpen

36e. Common variations in flute shape found in forged bowl gouges.

often results in fine cracks appearing in the end grain. The crisp appearance of the cut surface and edges is lost. This leaves the lifeless shape with irregularly rounded edges so characteristic of the amateur bowl turner.

A sharp scraper can be used to cut cleanly against the grain but only if it is used to take very thin shavings. To expect it to remove the required $\frac{1}{16}''$ or more of damaged wood is asking too much. Sharp scrapers become blunt scrapers very quickly and many sharpenings are required before the surface of the bowl is perfect. Also the scraper only has to 'catch' once and the surface is taken back to square one. To attempt to take a heavy cut with a scraper will damage the surface more than using the gouge.

I will attempt to explain a method of using a gouge to take finishing cuts with a slicing action. If a high-speed steel (HSS) gouge of correct design (and properly sharpened) is used, the method is easy to apply and can eliminate the rough patches entirely. The bowl then needs only light scraping and sanding before polishing.

If a carbon steel tool of the usual forged variety is used the result can be almost as good. But more skill is required and the limitations of the individual tool (which I will discuss later) can seriously limit the quality of the finish obtained with it.

Imagine a sharp knife used with a sawing action to take thin peelings off the stationary bowl. The slicing action of the blade will cut cleanly through the wood fibres leaving a perfect undisturbed surface. If the knife blade were to be pushed directly along without a slicing action it would lift out the wood fibres at points where it travels against the grain. The slicing or sawing motion is important in achieving the desired result. It helps the edge to cut cleanly.

It is impossible to cut a slice of bread with a single downward stroke of the knife through the loaf. It is similarly impossible to cut wood cleanly when the edge of the tool is pushed directly through the wood against the grain.

This causes the rough patches on the bowl (Fig 36b). The wood is revolving forcing the edge of the gouge directly into the grain and levering up the fibres. The bevel is rubbing as it should and the gouge is being fed slowly across the surface removing a fine shaving but leaving a terrible finish.

Now see Fig. 36c. This gouge is also being fed along the surface in the same path removing a fine shaving with the bevel rubbing to guide the tool. The difference is the angle with which the gouge is presented to the wood. The part of the cutting edge in contact with the wood is almost vertical.

As the motion of the wood surface is downward the part of the edge which is cutting is slicing sideways through the wood at high speed as well as being slowly pushed into it. Here we have the slicing action we require to give a perfect finish. It works. Try it.

The gouge must be properly sharpened with a straight or hollow ground bevel to give plenty of support. I use an edge angle of about 40°. The rest is placed as close as possible to the bowl to give maximum leverage and control. The slicing action is obtained with the gouge pointing slightly upwards so that the part of the edge in contact is at the proper angle (Fig. 36c). The bevel is made to rub as shown in the corresponding plan view (Fig. 36d) by moving the handle round sideways while keeping the angle in the vertical plane constant.

The purpose of rubbing the bevel is to guide the cutting edge and regulate the depth of cut. The bevel is made to bear on and to slide along the cut surface that the edge produces as the gouge is moved along. When the gouge is pushed it moves along the rest in a direction more or less parallel to the bevel, removing wood as it goes (Fig. 36d).

It is as if the bevel points in the direction the gouge will move when pushed. The handle must be swung round sideways away from the wood to increase the depth of cut or swung towards the wood, levering the edge away to decrease the depth of cut.

The angle, not the pressure, must be continuously regulated if the gouge is to take a cut of constant depth all the way round the curve of a bowl. During this cut round the bowl the end of the handle is kept at the same height. This keeps the cutting portion of the edge at the same angle to the vertical. Raising the handle would bring the cutting portion of the edge closer to vertical increasing the slicing effect.

This must not be overdone or the edge will be dulled very quickly. The effect of friction and rubbing on the edge when it is used to slice is severe and becomes extreme when the edge is too close to vertical.

A compromise is required if the edge is to survive even one trip around the bowl. I keep the edge about 20° from the vertical with a carbon steel gouge. The new high-speed steel bowl gouge made to my design by Henry Taylor (Tools) Ltd, The Forge, Lowther Road, Sheffield, has an advantage in that it is much more resistant to friction. Its edge can be brought 10° or so closer to the vertical and it will stay sharp 20 or 30 times as long as any carbon steel tool. For this reason the HSS gouge will give a better finish than a gouge made from carbon tool steel.

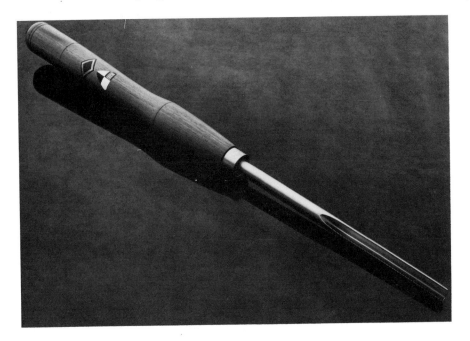

37. The new Superflute gouge in high speed steel made by Henry Taylor Tools, Sheffield.

Good results can be obtained from ordinary carbon steel tools provided certain precautions are taken. There is a risk with carbon steel that friction in cutting will result in overheating of the cutting edge and draw the temper making the edge soft and useless. HSS is immune to this because it will stand high temperatures without losing its temper.

38. The business end of the new gouge.

39. The smoothing action obtained by changing the angle of attack.

When a carbon steel tool is used the speed must not be too high and the bevel must not be rubbed too hard or the friction will be excessive. It is only necessary to rub the bevel lightly to keep the tool from jumping out of its groove. The amount of pressure required can only be learnt with practice.

It is necessary with carbon steel tools to roll the tool as it cuts. Many turners do this without knowing why. It involves slowly rotating the tool about its axis while keeping all the other angles, as previously described, the same. It sounds difficult but it only takes a little practice to learn. The effect is to change continuously the portion of the gouge which is cutting thus avoiding concentrating the heat and wear on one part of the edge for too long.

This helps to prevent burnt spots on the edge and makes the most of the steel available. Care must be taken not to dig the corner of the gouge into the wood or this can flip the tool over and cause a dig-in. Rolling the gouge can even go so far as to turn the tool upside down while still cutting correctly. Every part of the edge can be used before the gouge needs sharpening again.

Speed of the lathe must be a compromise. It must not be so high as to burn the tool or wear the edge away before it has time to cut. A very low speed makes the edge last much longer but cutting becomes tedious, especially on the finishing cuts. A low speed makes it easier for the gouge to ride up on the hard spots on the wood and to sink into the soft spots.

This causes a vibration which gets worse as the gouge moves along, unless the turner uses his 'feel' to anticipate the behaviour of the gouge and correct its movements before it gets out of control. A gouge is much easier to control at higher speed. Again an HSS gouge has a big advantage because it can be used at very high speed without fear of dulling the edge.

The principles and methods described apply to the inside of the bowl as well as the outside although rolling the gouge inside the bowl is only possible to a limited extent. However, complications arise when trying to obtain a good finish inside a bowl and the shape and design of the gouge itself becomes important.

Gouge Shape and Design

Controversy appears to exist over the correct type of gouge to use for bowl turning. Some turners favour a shallow fluted pointed nose gouge, others favour a deep fluted gouge ground straight across. I have done many cutting tests over the years trying the different shapes and styles of gouges in an effort to develop the ideal bowl gouge design. I have made my own tools to various designs on my small forge and I have a very strange collection of gouges on my tool rack. The result of all this experimentation is that I favour the deep fluted gouge with its edge ground straight across.

This type of gouge makes the most of the power available from the motor and so is faster for roughing-out the bowl. It is stronger and more rigid so is easier to control and safer to use inside the bowl where it has to stick out a long way over the tool rest. It is also more convenient for making slicing cuts at the finishing stage. It is awkward to get the cutting part of the edge to the required angle if a slicing cut with a pointed nose gouge is attempted.

The precise shape of the inside of the flute of the gouge is important. Unfortunately hand-forged gouges come out all different shapes, even when taken from the same batch from the same manufacturer. There are some that feel right and cut sweetly when you use them and there are some that don't. It is a matter of luck when you buy your gouge—unless you happen to know what to look for and how to pick out a good gouge from a batch of mediocre ones.

Some common faults in the sections found in forged bowl gouges are shown (Fig. 36e). Another point to look for is the strength of the tang. The gouge must not flex where it fits into its handle; otherwise full advantage cannot be taken of the leverage given by the long handle.

A good flute shape is like a French curve. It should have at some point on its edge a curvature which fits the job. When taking a cut inside a bowl with a good gouge the turner should be able to find a part of the edge which cuts sweetly, leaves a perfect finish, and makes the gouge controllable without chatter or vibration or any tendency to run off-course. Such ideal gouges are few and far between.

An alternative is to buy a set of three or four gouges of different sizes and curvatures. The one that fits the job best and handles well is used. Usually the roughing-out is done with a large gouge and the delicate finishing cuts with the smallest gouge in the set. But this is expensive and unnecessary as one gouge of the correct flute shape will do all the work well and out-perform the usual set of forged gouges in every respect.

As an experiment some years ago I had a gouge cut on a milling machine to the precise shape I wanted. Theoretically a machined gouge is not as good as a forged gouge in its edge-keeping quality because forging helps to improve the quality of the metal. However, this disadvantage was overcome by using a better grade of steel. The finished result was a gouge superior to a forged gouge in every respect, including the keenness of its edge. No tang was left on the end. Instead the solid bar was sunk deep into the handle giving a strong and rigid tool with all the necessary leverage.

The tool was such a success that we went into production. The machined gouges have the same shape all the way along the flute and of course all the gouges are the same.

8. Flat Work

Table Tops, Cheese and Breadboards, Plates

The making of a wine-table top is described as a typical example of how a flat surface is achieved. These tops vary in size from miniatures of 9″ to those 2′ in diameter. They are mounted on a turned central pedestal, supported at the bottom by a tripod of short curved legs. The popular wood is mahogany, and the top is from stock 1″ thick.

One easy way of ensuring a flat surface, say where a plain breadboard is being fashioned, is to use stock, thicknessed and planed both sides so that only the edge needs turning to shape. However, in the case of the wine-table, the flat surface has to be recessed in order to allow for a beaded rim, so here planed wood is of no advantage.

Screw Fitting

Screws can be a nuisance when comparatively thin wood has to be turned. Very short screws, thicker the better, should be used, and every care taken in screwing the wood to the faceplate. Every thread has to count, and there is no place here for the 'Birmingham screwdriver' (a hammer) starting the screw.

It is quite easy for a turner, experienced or not, to take just that little too much wood from the face and thus go through into the screw points. If this is done when the gouge is being used to remove waste then it is clumsy work and inexcusable, but it can be accepted as just unfortunate if the penetration occurs during final scraping. A trained ear can pinpoint the exact moment when the scraper touches metal instead of wood. There is a distinct 'click', and on hearing this the lathe should be stopped immediately. It is my experience, and I have never discovered the reason why, but even though the screws used are all of the same length, only one is hit first and the metal exposed through the wood. That is, of course, if the lathe is stopped at the first click. This fact makes a repair job quite simple. The work, with faceplate attached, is removed from the lathe and the offending screw taken out, a little more metal snipped from the damaged point, and the shortened screw replaced in position. One at a time the other screws are removed, shortened and replaced. This ensures that the position of the faceplate is not disturbed. The shortened screws will allow just enough margin for the table top to be surfaced and sanded and, with luck, the only sign of damage may be one very small 'pinhole', which, when filled with stopper, is invisible under the finish.

To revert back to bowl turning, this kind of damage can similarly occur when too ambitious in endeavouring to make as deep a bowl as possible out of the depth of wood available. An experienced turner uses his fingers caliper fashion and develops an instinct as to how far to go when hollowing out, but for the amateur, a good depth guide can be made up as shown in the drawing. It can be made from a piece of batten, say $1\frac{1}{2}'' \times \frac{1}{2}''$ thick, long enough to span the largest bowl, and with a $\frac{3}{8}''$ hole bored through the centre. In this hole is a sliding-fit short piece of pointed dowel marked off in $\frac{1}{8}''$ length divisions. As an example, say the screws of the faceplate penetrate the bottom of a $4''$ thick disc by $\frac{3}{8}''$. Then the maximum inside depth of the bowl can only be $3\frac{5}{8}''$. The dowel marker of the depth guide is adjusted to protrude $3\frac{1}{2}''$ through the batten, and the depth of the bowl tested at intervals during turning until the point of the dowel just clears the bottom of the bowl, with the batten resting across the rim.

It has been known for an enthusiast, with his gouge correctly bevelled and making the shavings fly for the first time, to be overcome by his new-found mastery of toolwork and go right through the centre of the bowl into the faceplate before he comes back to his senses. There is hope even in these extreme circumstances.

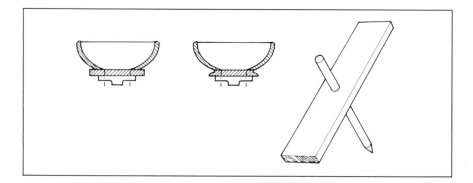

40. Repair of damaged bowl.

The severely damaged bowl is given first aid by means of a glued-on addition of a base plinth. A suitable piece of wood, either the same as the bowl or of a contrasting species, is glued over the bottom. A very fine drill is used to drill through the centre of the original screw holes from the inside of the bowl and into the plinth. This provides locating holes in the base of the plinth so that the faceplate can be fixed to it and the whole assembly centrally remounted. The damage inside the bowl is removed and blended into the wood of the plinth, the outside shaped and similarly blended, and an expensive piece of wood has been salvaged.

Fixing without Screws

One reliable method is by a glue-and-brownpaper joint. Scrapwood, it can be ply, blockboard, deal, etc., is screwed to a faceplate, turned and faced flat. It is then covered with a piece of thick brown paper glued to the face with hot Scotch glue, or with any simple brown animal glue. Modern adhesives are to be avoided. Glue is also spread over the face of the brown paper and the stock to be turned is cramped to this face and all left for the glue to set hard. This joint will then stand considerable pressure while the work is being turned. When finished, the paper joint is partly split with the aid of a razor blade or knife and the work forcibly wrenched off the scrapwood disc. A layer of brown paper will be left adhering to the base of the turned work and this is removed by a sponge and hot water. A modern adhesive may not be so easily removed.

Table Top

The wood for the wine-table is sawn to required diameter and screwed or fixed to a faceplate. Where the size is too large for it to swing without hitting part of the lathe bed, the faceplate can sometimes be packed out by means of a scrap disc and so allow clearance.

When it is so large that the actual hand-rest assembly gets in the way, there may be some means of removing the assembly and mounting it separately, either in a separate tripod stand, or by improvisation in a vice on the bench, the bench being brought up to the work.

The edge is turned truly circular using a ½″ bowl-turning gouge in the same way as when chipping down a bowl disc to round. The edge of the table top is then slightly rounded towards the faceplate. This has the effect of making the wood look thicker than it actually is. Then the rest is taken round to the front and the top faced, i.e. levelled with the ⅜″ gouge for a width of about 2″ from the edge towards the centre. Just enough wood is

41a. *Wine table top.*
The mahogany disc has been turned true at the edge and rounded off towards the faceplate. The front has been levelled (faced) for a short distance inwards, and the corner of a light scraping tool is being used to cut down the right-hand side of a square bead.

41b. Parting tool being used to cut down the left-hand side of a square bead. The parting tool is 'waggled' slightly from side to side to give it ample clearance in which to work and scrape out to required depth.

removed to level the surface—this can be tested while revolving by trailing the finger tips against it. The ultra cautious can stop the lathe and just look.

A square bead or ridge is put into the rim with either a sharp parting tool, used scraper fashion, or with the corner of a light scraping tool. When beading or otherwise embellishing turned work, the decoration should always be over-emphasised, i.e. larger and deeper than intended for the finished result. Papering, however carefully done, will always reduce the decoration to a slight degree and this must be allowed for in the initial cutting. The corners of the square bead are very carefully rounded off with a scraper, then the remainder of the disc is recessed by removing waste with the ½″ bowl gouge, relying on the eye to keep it as level as possible. The recessed top is further levelled with the aid of a heavy domed scraper, remembering to adjust the height of the rest so that the cutting edge points down on contact with the wood, working from centre pip outwards. The level of the top can now frequently be tested with a suitable length of wood straight-edge, and high points taken down. The final touches are made

41c. The corners of the square bead have been lightly rounded over. The long and strong ½″ bowl gouge is removing waste and deepening the centre. The area next to the bead is left flat for a short distance. Note the *right* hand pushing the gouge, the blade on its side and cutting with the centre-to-left-hand edge. The dangerous right-hand trailing point is well clear, the leading point at the left is almost but not quite touching the wood to obtain maximum width of cutting edge. The gouge handle is down and inclined to the right so that the bevel of the gouge is rubbing the wood.

41d. Using a heavy domed scraper and long rest to further level the bottom, working from centre outwards. The domed cutting edge (see photograph of set of scraping tools) will only allow a short length of edge to cut at one time. Frequent testing with a wood straight edge will show up areas to be levelled off. Note the 'under-blade' grip.

41e. An area at the centre has been accurately flattened using a 1" wide straight-across scraper. The heavy straight-across scraper is now being used to 'spread' this flat outwards. Note that it must be used pointing *well* down, so the rest has to be correspondingly heightened.

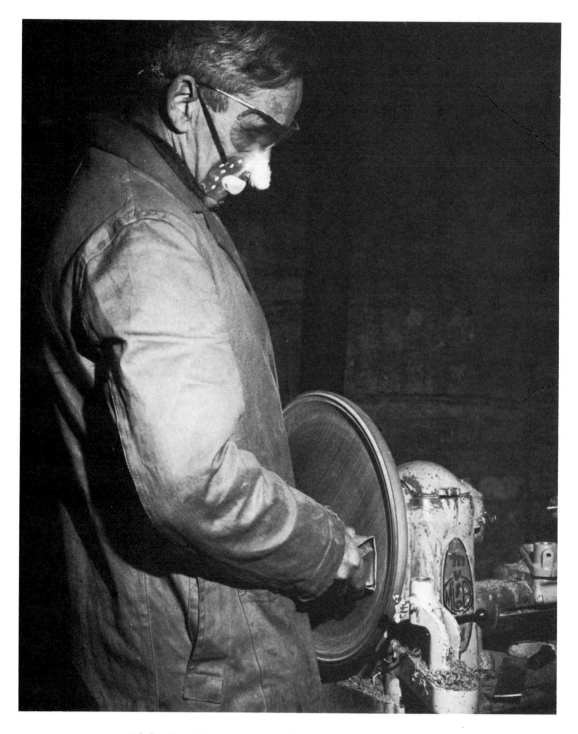

41f. Sanding flat, using open-coat garnet round cork block. Note protection from dust afforded by goggles and nurses' light-weight mask. Mahogany dust is very fine and can irritate.

with a scraper that is ground straight across, one of small width first, followed by the widest available.

The small scraper is applied to the very centre of the disc, cutting at *exact* centre height, and placed so that the middle of the scraper is across the centre point of the disc. A little thought will make it plain that in this position only half of the scraper will do any cutting, since the wood at left of centre (or right—depending on type of lathe and rotation) is revolving the other way and the other side of the scraper can only rub. In fact the only way to make any impression on the wood at all is to have the rest raised very high indeed so that the square scraper is pointing down to the centre at a pronounced angle and then it is actually *pushed* into the wood at first and taken slightly across and back again, repeatedly, until a flat is made a little larger than the width of the scraper. The fact that the scraper is continually being taken to the side of the wood where it will not cut, and then transferred to the cutting side, ensures that a flat spot is made that is really level without 'pimple' or 'dimple'. When this has been accomplished, the widest scraper is used to spread this flat across the surface of the disc until it meets the rim. The side of the flat scraper will remove wood provided it is not too thick in depth. If it is, the excess is nibbled away with the scraper by pushing it in and then reverting to the sideways traverse again. It is of great help to endeavour to scrape only with the very centre of the straight scraper. This, of course, cannot be accomplished, but the idea behind it tends to keep the scraper edge parallel with the face of the wood. If reverse is available, any disturbed grain can be calmed down by applying a light straight scraper across the disc, cutting in reverse rotation.

Tools for Faceplate Work—Bowls, Hollow-ware, etc.

A full modern set of bowl turning tools consists of one high-speed steel gouge, supplemented by six heavy duty scrapers, now made in solid high-speed steel by the same firm, Henry Taylor Tools, and possibly two hand-held high-speed steel bars about 1½″ × ⅛″ thick, up to 1′ long, ground straight across or skew. There are many grades of high-speed steel, some better than others. The gouge made by Henry Taylor bears the brand name Diamic, and also the approval of the Design Centre, London. The solid high-speed steel scrapers bear the same brand name.

9. Turning Between Centres: Tools

Nearly all the rules can be made to go by the board when turning between centres (spindle turning), and it is a pity. The beginner at woodturning usually starts by experimenting on his own with a piece of wood held between the fork-driving centre and tailstock centre, thus 'turning between centres'. Trying to handle the tools according to the books, he may be lucky in applying them more or less correctly, and from thereon he improves rapidly. On the other hand, and it is a fairly even chance, he may misinterpret the written instructions and come to grief, or use the tools in a crude scraping position and thereby manage to produce something from his efforts, but will always complain about the lack of a decent finish. And he will never be able to turn out a well-finished bowl using the bad habits he has acquired. My course syllabus, very elastic, depending upon the aims or abilities of the pupil concerned, always starts with the most difficult tool to understand and to work with, the long and strong deep fluted bowl turning gouge. This is contrary to the teaching principle that depends on beginning with the easy stuff and progressing to the more difficult. Turning between centres is easy work.

The bowl gouge is the *master* tool in turnery, because using it properly brings into effect *all* the right principles of tool-work in turnery, correct angles, bevel application, footwork, cutting into wood as opposed to scraping it off, and true application which develops a craftsman woodturner and not an inferior 'scraper'. Undergoing tuition, a pupil, depending on natural aptitude, may have to spend up to a full day with the gouge alone, but after this, never needs more than a couple of hours on spindle work before he or she is using every tool that can be used between centres, using them properly and enjoying the experience. So my advice to beginners is to

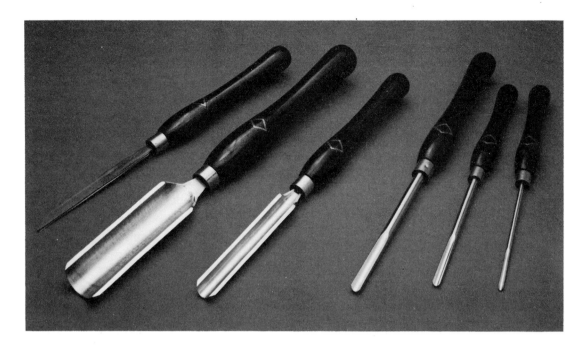

42. Three spindle gouges—¼"; ⅜"; ½"
Two roughing-out gouges—¾"; 1½"
Roy Child fluted parting tool.

43. Plain parting tool, two beading and parting tools ⅜"; ¼".
Two chisels—square-across and skew—1¼".
One ½" skew chisel.

practise as much as they can with the bowl gouge, and if they find they are dissatisfied with their work between centres, go back to the long and strong, and turn out another bowl!

Roughing-out Gouges

The advice given in some books recommending that lengths of wood for turning should first be rounded, or at least the corners taken off, before being placed in the lathe, causes great amusement in the trade. We have a machine that does this job. It is called a lathe. We also have a tool specifically designed for rounding down squares of wood in the lathe and it is called a roughing-out gouge.

The section of the gouge is a complete half-round, not a U shape, and the edge is ground straight across as in a bowl-turning gouge, but despite its massive appearance it is not in any way suitable for bowl turning. The bevel is a short one, 45 degrees or thereabouts, and a very good working edge can be put on with just the aid of a grindstone and a gentle touch. There is no need to remove the burr that will be raised on the inside.

The reason for grinding the edge straight across, unlike all other gouges used for spindle turning, which have a rounded nose (lady's fingernail), is

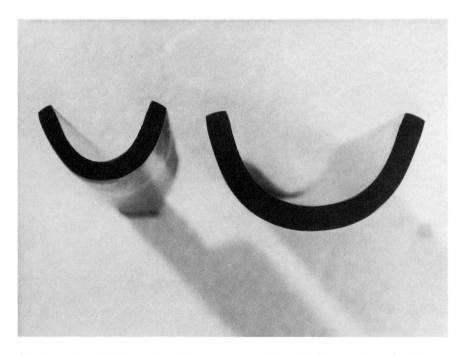

44a. Deep fluted half-round roughing-out gouges ¾" and 1½". Front view showing half-round section (not shallow fluted), and short bevels.

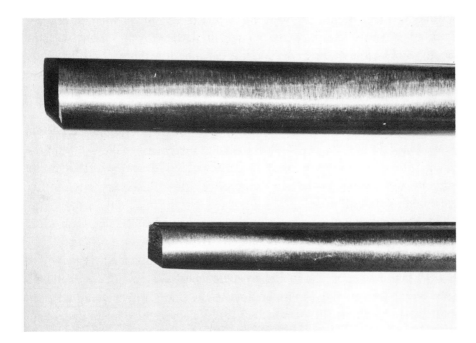

44b. Side view showing short bevels 45 degrees hollow ground.

44c. Plan view showing edge ground straight-across (the only type of gouge used between centres that is not rounded edged).

so that *all* the edge can be used by rolling it across the work during the removal of waste wood. A 1½″ gouge, if flattened out, would measure nearly 3″ of usable cutting edge, so it is capable of making a lot of shavings fly before the need for re-sharpening. A 6″ × 6″ square of wood, however long, can be taken down to a smooth cylinder before a circular saw could even remove the corners!

Using the more commonly available shallow fluted gouge to take wood down to a cylinder can result in an irregular wavy surface being left on the wood. The half-round section of the roughing gouge leaves a straight and smooth surface which can be so good as not to require any further treatment with a chisel.

There is also the great advantage that the chances of digging-in are very remote and very little practice is needed before any beginner is completely confident and proficient in its use. In fact, there is only one rule to adhere to, and that is to apply the tool at an angle where the bevel has a chance to rub, and not at an angle like 90 degrees to the wood, which would result in a scraping action, in other words the handle is always held lower down than the edge.

Long and Strong, Straight-across Chisel

A chisel is the tool which most amateurs distrust, and are thoroughly frightened of using, yet after ten minutes of practical instruction and demonstration, most of the fear has gone, and they are removing shavings quite happily if not completely competently. There is no magic employed in my teaching. The chisel is a simple cutting tool and performs its task as well as any other, provided certain simple basic principles are understood in its operation. There cannot be a more elementary principle in use of tools than making sure they are kept sharp. Yet this is a common failing in most beginners. A sharp turning chisel does a great deal of work in a very short time indeed, and this can be a trap. A cabinet-maker, working with a chisel at his bench, soon knows when resharpening is required, and, in comparison with a turning chisel, nothing like the amount of work has been done when the resharpening stage is reached. Yet a beginner expects far more production out of a turning chisel, so most of the time he is working with a blunt, therefore unpredictable, tool. A second principle is that to keep an edge sharp as long as possible it must be cutting *into* wood and not scraping along the outside, so, like the gouge, the bevel must rub. The most obvious scraping angle is when presented level and to the side of the wood being turned, and it should be obvious that the sharp edge, presented thus, is immediately scraped blunt in the first few revolutions.

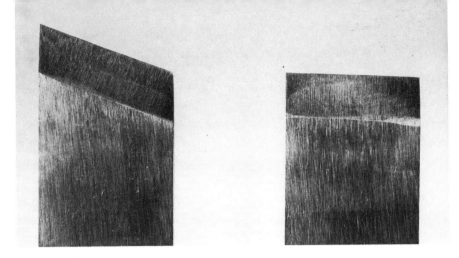

45a. Long and strong 1¼″ long-cornered (skew) and straight-across chisels.

45b. Side view of angled skew and straight-across chisels. Note length of hollow-ground bevels. Point of long-cornered chisel to be maintained 'as new'.

What is not so simply understood is the fact that even with the bevel rubbing and some shavings being removed it is possible that the edge is still being blunted in a very short space of time. This is because the angle of cutting is not *deep* enough, and the wood is being more rubbed with the edge than cut. To put it another way, the removal of a very fine shaving of wood may have more blunting effect than if a thicker shaving is being taken off. I am working hard to get this point home, and, as I have mentioned before, one 'talking-practical-demonstration' of a few minutes would save hundreds of words, but perhaps another example will get the message across. We have all had the domestic task of splitting firewood with the kitchen axe. Consider the edge of this humble tool. Once it has penetrated the wood, the sides of the blade do the work and the edge has a free journey down the billet. It is, in fact, apart from initial entry, not doing much work at all, therefore remains keen longer. I'm much keener myself when I've less to do.

Now consider the section of a chisel. You will realise that I prefer a long-and-strong, and mine is more than ¼″ thick in the blade. This gives me a benefit of weight (to combat vibration of wood and lathe) and strength at the edge to give me good backing for the actual edge itself. It is also 1¼″ or 2″ wide. We used to get up to 4″ wide at one time, but these are uncommon and not all that necessary, and, as a fellow turner has said, if you can use one that width to its full capacity then send this book back for an immediate refund of the purchase price.

Using a thin-bladed chisel instead of a thick heavy one can be compared with sharpening a pencil, either with a fragile razor blade, or a sturdy penknife. The razor blade will bend and quiver, but the knife stolidly cuts away. Right tool for the job?

There are still tool-makers who produce woodturning chisels with bevels beautifully curving from each side to meet at the edge. Bevels are also called 'cannels' and this cannelling is still hand-done and apparently easier to do curved than flat. Whatever it is designed for, and I have yet to find out, a rounded cutting bevel is completely useless in woodturnery (and anything else?). The bevels should be absolutely flat, or, ideally, completely opposite to the manufactured ones, hollow-ground.

The angle of bevel I prefer, and have the factory grind for me, is 30 degrees, a little longer than some of my fellows in the trade, but it suits me. Woodturning is a very individual craft, and the individuals, after some years, get quite individual ideas regarding their tools!

A good position for grinding chisels is on top of the edge of the stone, support at a constant angle being aided by the long handle tucked under the arm. The object is to grind the bevel hollow from base of bevel almost up to the edge. A 6″ diameter grindstone gives a good hollow-ground finish. It looks professional if the bevels on both sides are ground to the same length, but this is not essential, since the chisel is actually two tools in one. The final honing is done with a medium or fine grade oilstone, followed by stropping on a piece of leather similar to a barber's strop, only the leather is glued on to a block of wood and treated occasionally with crocus powder and light oil. The edge should be as keen as experience and patience can get it. There is no second sharpening bevel as in a firmer chisel.

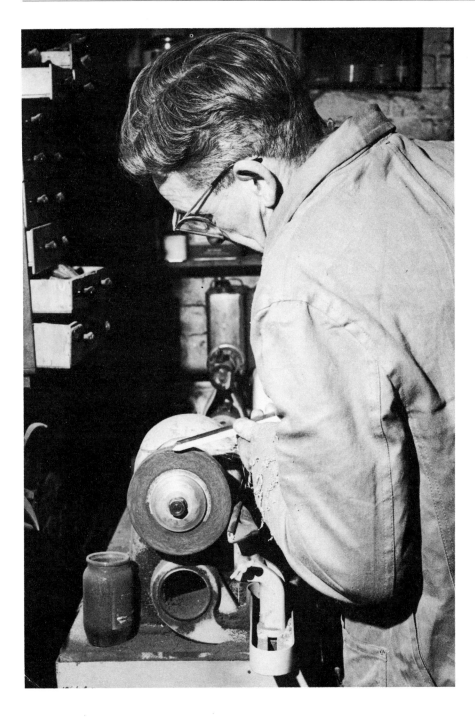

46. Grinding a long and strong straight-across chisel, long handle held firmly under arm-pit.
Hollow-ground bevel formed from bottom up to cutting edge.
Tool moved from side to side. Goggles.

47. Honing a long and strong straight-across chisel. Long handle is wedged firmly upright against headstock. Pressure of both hands towards each other to keep stone flat against bevel. Chisel held still, stone moving. Black line of oil on edge shows that stone is cutting. Chisel sharpened from both sides. Frequent honing very necessary.

48. Stropping a sharpened long and strong skew chisel to remove rag. Edge beginning to flatten out hollow-ground bevel. Almost due for re-grinding.

The reason why so much use of the skew chisel advocated in articles and books is due to the ignorance of the existence and proper use of the roughing-out gouge. The beginner is told to round down the wood with a pointed nose spindle gouge, and since there is no way he can avoid leaving a ridged surface by using this wrong tool, a finishing chisel *has* to be used to get a finished result. When learning correct use of the straight-across chisel, proceed as follows, assuming a cut from right to left if you are a right-hander. With the lathe at rest, angle the blade so that the middle of the cutting edge is in contact with the wood just below top dead centre of the cylinder. This means that the tool rest must be raised to support the chisel blade. The tool handle will therefore be uncomfortably high. With the lathe still at rest, push the blade along to the left and take a very small curl of a shaving with the very centre of the cutting edge. Note that one corner of the short side of the blade is the *only* contact between blade and rest. If any pressure, consciously or otherwise, is placed on the blade by the left hand, smooth progress along the tool rest can be inhibited by the sharp corner, and gives rise to a jerky cut. The left hand could as well be in your pocket, or holding a cigarette, for all the good it does. The right hand holding the handle does all the work, but needs the support of the body, so it is held firmly to the side of the body, with the legs spread out and the whole of the body moves along as the cut proceeds. Start the lathe and now use the centre of the edge to give you the insignificant little shaving that you got before, this time under power. Alter the angle of the blade to give a better shaving by moving the handle more to the left. Do not allow the leading point to cut, but gradually bring it round until there is a decent shaving coming off and the trailing edge or point is dangerously close to contact. When it does touch, and during practice it is bound to, you will be made aware of it quite clearly! Have a look at the photographs on pages 112–3, and this will help to explain the text.

An amateur can quite easily use a chisel the proper way, then finds the finish nothing like what he expects, so is puzzled and doubts his ability. The fault may not be his, but in the grain of the timber he is using. If he tried to plane the same timber in the same direction in a vice in the bench, the keenest plane blade would wreak the same damage. A lathe is only a machine and cannot reverse the natural laws. It would be best in this case to leave the chisel alone and get the best possible finish with a gouge instead.

For simple practice and enjoyment with the chisel, a straight-grained defect-free piece of pine, or similar in beech that is perfectly green (unseasoned), is ideal timber to work on, and the longed for shavings should soon come off, leaving a polished finish on the wood. Good for the ego.

I mentioned in bowl turning that a woodturner's position is an unnatural one for a beginner, and what is normally considered to be the right position, e.g. in joinery work, is unsuitable. This error can be carried over in turning between centres, especially when a chisel is being used. A joiner's bench is at a much lower height than wood mounted in the usual lathe. When wood is being planed in the vice, we are well over the top of it, and able to exert pressure downwards without really being conscious of doing so. When the beginner starts using a chisel on wood in the lathe he assumes the same attitude and holds the handle at the same angle as he would hold a plane. He traverses the wood, with bevel rubbing, sometimes so hard that the wood is almost scorched, but no shavings come off, and the chisel edge 'skates' along the surface. All he needs to be told is to lift the handle UP into an uncomfortable position close to the armpit, and lo and behold the chisel commences to slice merrily away. We could have the lathe lower, of course, but this would have an adverse effect when faceturning, so the heights of most lathes are a compromise.

Another amateur fault is that he traverses the chisel far too rapidly along the wood, possibly anxious to reach the end safely. Most of us know that when using a machine planer, the slower we push wood over the blades the cleaner and more ripple-free the surface, so it should be obvious that a slow traverse with the chisel over revolving wood will give us the same result. Yet another fault is *too much* pressure of the chisel on wood, even though only a thin shaving is coming off. The wood in a lathe is only held at each end, and there is empty space underneath. It is easy to 'bend' the wood down with excessive pressure so that it is taken out of true revolution and tries to climb up the chisel blade, causing ribbing, which is like a coarse screwthread rippling along the surface.

Ribbing is often encountered when long lengths of wood, or very thin spindles, are being turned. This will be discussed later and various remedies can be tried.

Long and Strong Skew (Long-Cornered) Chisel

The straight-across chisel is moved in one plane, i.e. with the broad side of the blade parallel to the floor. The skew is never used flat, always in an axe-like movement, long corner entering the wood first and the cut continued by *lifting* the handle, not just pushing the point in.

The point is used to lead in a slicing cut when we are cleaning up end-grain. It is also used to start pummels or squares that are left in turned work such as chair legs and rails etc. Another use is in clean parting off work where the same result from a parting tool would be too rough for the finished product. The small skew chisel is used in instances where the larger one is too clumsy to handle. In the absence of a long and strong beading and parting tool, the small chisel can also be used to cut beads.

Parting Tool

This is hollow-ground (see photograph on page 101), and new ones are waisted to allow clearance at the sides. This is entirely a metal-man's idea, as he envisages the tool being used to part off metal, and clearance in this is definitely needed. In wood, we need no such precaution, as the slightest wiggle of the blade during the process of the cut gives us all the clearance we need! So when the waist is ground away by use, there is no need to rush out and buy another tool. Mine is so old that I am almost using the tang. It is used for completely severing wood, for preliminary marking out in template or copy work, for part removal of waste wood ready for follow-up work by gouge or chisel. It can take the place of a beading tool in making small beads, and it can be used for cleaning up small areas of wood by traversing the surface back and forth, since it is too small in width to incur any dig-in damage. When used to penetrate wood, it is advisable to start by having the tool horizontal to the centre side of the cylinder and pushing the blade in, i.e. a scraping action. This gives a clean entry into the wood without furring or splintering the sides of the cut, but in order to preserve the sharp edge, it should not be pushed in too deeply. To deepen the cut, the next step is to raise the edge so that it is resting almost on top of the cut, the handle being correspondingly lowered. The fingers holding the blade on the hand-rest grip firmly and act as a pivot, and the cut is deepened by raising up the handle. Never get the blade under the gradually decreasing diameter of the cut area.

Long and Strong Beading and Parting Tool
These used to be available in the tool catalogues but seem to have disappeared now, but they are so useful that I have them made specially. The section is about ¼″ or ⅜″ square, and the top cutting edge is hollow ground similar to a parting tool. The other end has a normal tang, so I cannot see where they can be difficult to make. A long and strong ¼″ square across chisel is a substitute, but not so handy in use. Employed as a plain parting tool in the same way as described, it gives a wider cut where this is needed, and is also effective in deep parting off large diameter cylinders or, for instance, in 'squaring-up' the base of a large diameter table lamp base. The extra strength, thickness, and weight of the tool helps to stop it 'shivering' as more and more length is pushed over the hand-rest and is without support. Also, like the plain parting tool, it can be used to

49a. Long and strong beading and parting tool, and plain parting tool. View showing edge. Note waisting of side of parting tool.

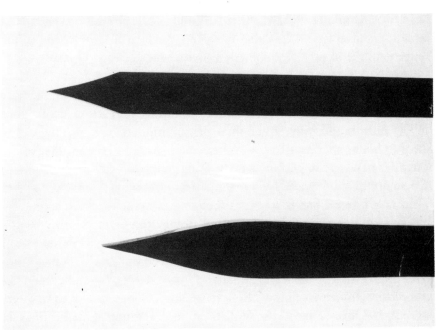

49b. Long and strong beading and parting tool, and parting tool. View showing hollow-ground bevels.

50. 'Squaring-up' the end of large diameter work with the long and strong beading and parting tool. The cut has been started at a scraping angle, then up in a slight arc which will then continue down towards the revolving tail centre. The extra section thickness of the long and strong stops any sideways whip of the tool, however far it protrudes over the supporting rest.

clean up small surface areas, since it is still not quite wide enough to be liable to incur a dig-in. It is also extremely good for turning beads, much better than the skew chisel sometimes advocated for this purpose.

Gouges for Turning Hollows between Centres

A set of three (¼″, ½″, ¾″) will suffice for most work, each being used for hollow finishing slightly larger than the appropriate size of gouge. Any coves or hollows larger than ¾″ can easily be made by one or other of the roughing-out gouges, so that larger spindle gouges are not really required. Although it is quite possible to make a wide hollow using a ¼″ gouge this takes longer and is bad practice, as the result is never clean enough. Long and strong tools are NOT recommended, they can be too clumsy in use. Once again, some tool-makers have their own ideas as to the shape of woodturning tools, and it seems a pity that woodturners will simply not agree and insist on reshaping them. So the gouges could be supplied ground straight across and we have to spend our time in regrinding them 'nosed', i.e. like a lady's fingernail. Mine are bitten, possible due to frustration.

The bevels can be quite long, much longer than bowl-turning gouges, and a shallow flute is quite acceptable. I grind the bevels hollow by using the grindstone and swivelling the gouge end about so that the edge is always uppermost on the stone. Being good at it I can stop just as the sparks reach the edge, leaving a tiny burr on the metal.

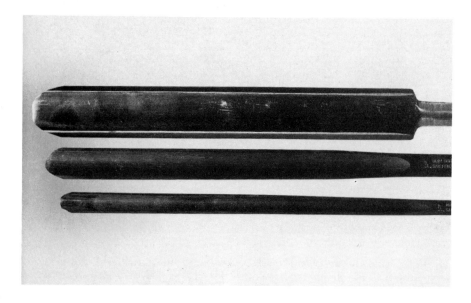

51. Set of spindle turning gouges ¾″; ½″; ¼″. Shallow fluted, rounded noses.

52. Honing a spindle gouge. Both hands controlling stone flat against bevel. Gouge rotated against stone during sharpening.

For a beginner it is strongly recommended that the final sharp edge is obtained with the use of a flat oilstone rubbing on the bevel, the inside rag being removed by a curved slip. However, the bevel must be kept FLAT at all costs, and careless use of the oilstone will very soon produce a rounded effect.

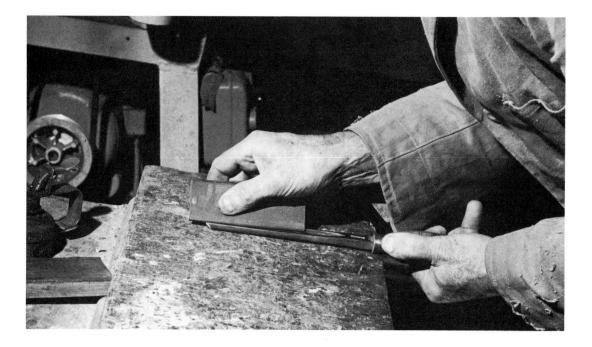

53. Removing inside rag with curved slip. Gouge held down on bench, considerable pressure being used on slip, but care taken not to 'round-over'. Inside flute must remain flat.

The gouges can also be used to round the wood, say a ball shape, as well as hollowing out. This operation is the same as in turning the outside round of a bowl, the whole of the bevel resting on the wood, the handle brought upwards until the edge starts to cut, and the rounding effected by *rolling* the gouge to the side required, bringing up the handle at the same time. The more pronounced the roll, the more rounded the result.

A long and strong deep fluted ⅜″ gouge ground with a pointed nose is an extra useful tool for between centres work, and sometimes in place of a bowl gouge for doing small hollow ware. It is not recommended for use on large bowls. When turning boxes and containers between centres (see later), the pointed gouge gets a grip on the end grain waste and is then used to cut it away. The standard strength spindle gouge is just not strong enough for the hard work it has to do.

Calipers

These are an essential tool for checking the diameter of a cylinder of wood. The calipers I prefer are those provided with a firm screw-setting adjustment. The cheaper variety with plain friction-held arms are not so reliable, as when testing wood which is revolving they can easily be sprung

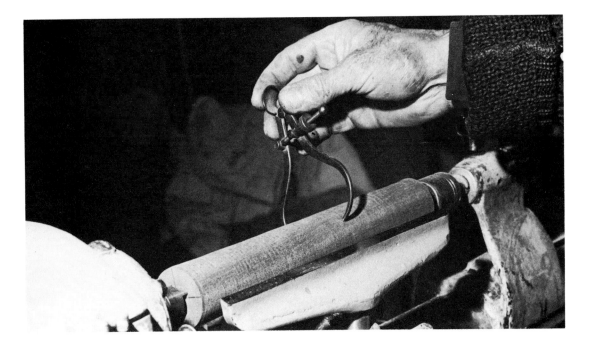

54. Position of calipers when testing revolving wood.

from the set position and open to a larger diameter without the user's knowledge. Diameters can be frequently tested on the revolving wood until the caliper legs just slide over. Two precautions are necessary. The wood must be already turned to a full cylinder prior to any testing, otherwise projecting corners could catch the legs and wrench them away from the holder. When applying the calipers, the legs should point *towards* the user, i.e. approaching from the back of the wood. Any unforeseen snag will then take the calipers away from the user and they will not be liable to catch in the tool rest.

10. Turning Between Centres: General Practice

The best way to start learning to turn wood properly between centres is not to make anything at all; and I'm not Irish bred. A 2″ sawn square of wood about 10″ long is not expensive, even today, and it can be of any common variety, softwood if you like. There is no need to order rosewood. The primary object is to use the tools; the ultimate result can be a matchstick, that is if you are good enough to get that far without complete destruction occurring long beforehand.

Diagonal lines are drawn from corner to corner across both ends of the wood to find the centres. One end will be driven by the lathe headstock, using a pronged driving centre. The other will be supported by a dead cup or ring centre, plain cone centre, or if you are affluent, the much preferred live revolving centre. The most common driving centre has a middle point and two prongs. The prongs are short 'blades' like small chisels, one side of each is flat, the opposite ones bevelled and *sharpened* at 45 degrees. The middle point and the bevels of the blades must be buried firmly into the wood at one end so that the timber can be driven. A lot of centres I have encountered in school lathes are in a deplorable condition, battered and scarred, and have obviously never been sharpened from new. They could never drive wood unless the timber was forcibly squeezed between centres and only held by excessive friction.

I have at least two driving centres, one which remains in the headstock, and a spare handy on the bench. This is used to hammer (soft hammer) into the wood and then withdrawn so that the timber can be transferred to the lathe to fit nicely into the driving centre that is already there. It is inadvisable to mount the wood in the lathe without doing this, because otherwise the tailstock has to be screwed up hard so that the driving centre

55. Revolving tail centre and four-prong driving centre in position in lathe.

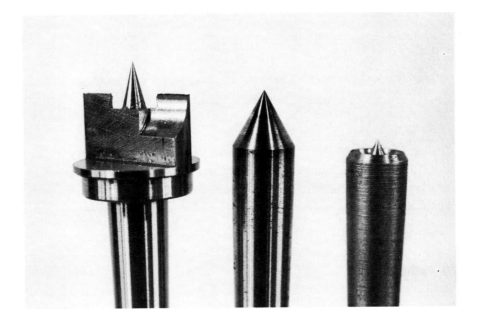

56. Two-prong driving centre, cone tail centre, cup tail centre.

prongs can penetrate sufficiently to get a good purchase. The wood is then too tightly held between centres, can whip when being turned down to small diameter, and there will be trouble with the dead centre burning due to excessive pressure.

The middle point of the prong chuck is usually far too long as supplied. Since all it has to do is help centre the wood, it can, with no lack of efficiency, be shortened considerably with a small triangular file while it is revolving at slow speed in the headstock. It will then offer less resistance when being driven into the wood. A hardened four pronged driving centre can be obtained. This gives double the drive and is less liable to split the end grain of small section timber. A further help to avoid splitting is instead of drawing the lines across the ends, they are sawn to a depth of ⅛″, the driving blades will then have a better purchase.

With a plain tail centre, this needs a spot of oil or grease as lubrication and reduces friction so that clouds of blue smoke do not erupt. This is not needed if a revolving centre is used, as the supporting cone is in ball bearings and revolves with the wood. A cheap revolving centre has a certain amount of end play in these bearings; the best and most expensive version has none at all.

Height of Rest

I am a little mystified as to why I am asked so often about this. It is not really the height of the rest that matters, but at what height the tool edge enters the wood. This will vary with the thickness of the tool, type of tool, viz. the trimming chisel needs to work on top of the wood. If the rest is too low, the tool can be made to cut correctly by lowering the handle.

Anyway, to start off with, have the rest at a height so that the tool used is cutting just above centre of the wood. To obtain some idea before ultimately experience does the teaching, and this does not take very long, vary the heights experimentally between extremes and see how it works. The comfortable, therefore correct, height will soon become apparent.

Speed of Lathe

Here again, we are not too fussy, as long as it is not so obviously too fast for the diameter of wood being turned as to make the whole lathe vibrate. A very good way of learning, each time a different diameter of timber is being used, is to have the lathe at lowest speed, take some trial cuts, raise to next speed, have another go, and so on. After all, on most lathes-cum-combination machines, there is only the choice of the three lowest speeds, the fastest being reserved for grinding, sawing, routing, etc. Broadly speaking, the speed should not be so low as to make turning off shavings slow and laborious, or so fast that there is no time for shavings to develop.

Roughing Down from the Square

The 2″ square length of wood is placed between centres, the rest adjusted say just below centre height and at a distance so that the corners of the wood just clear it when being revolved by hand. The lathe is started. By standing back a little, there will be seen a distinct shadow, a sort of mirage effect, caused by the rotation of the corners of the wood. An ordinary shaded light situated behind the lathe will show this up distinctly. Fluorescent lights close to the lathe are to be avoided, they tend to dispel these shadows. Beneath this shadow is a more solid shape. This is the size of the cylinder when the corners have been completely turned off. When standing closer to the lathe in the position required to use the tools, the shadow tends to disappear from view, leaving only the 'solid', and here the beginner makes his first mistake by attempting to attack the 'solid', without first disposing of the 'shadow'. The result can be an awful splintering, very bad for the nerves. Thinking this out, it might possibly be one reason for all the advice given to take off the corners first by sawing or planing.

The best approach is to 'feel' for the corners with the centre cutting edge of the roughing-out gouge, held with flute directly uppermost. The handle

57a. Roughing down a length of wood that was originally a rectangular section. The cutting is still being accomplished by the centre of the gouge traversing both ways. As the wood becomes more rounded it is easy to roll the gouge over from side to side as it traverses, thus using different parts of the whole cutting edge and removing thick shavings. Note that the gouge is inclined upwards at a bevel-rubbing angle.

57b. The wood has been roughly rounded to a cylinder, and now the gouge is being used in a different way to smooth and level the surface. The centre of the left-hand edge is cutting only, and the gouge in this position is being moved from left to right. The gouge cannot dig in.

is held well down, the blade firmly on the rest, and the tool pushed forward slowly until it just makes contact with the corners of the revolving wood. It will jolt just a little, not to any frightening degree, and small chips come flying off. Holding the gouge still at this contact angle, it is traversed back and forth along the wood, the handle coming up a little each time until a stage is reached when most of the corners have been well rounded down, and then further removal of wood is ridiculously easy and most enjoyable.

It must be remembered that the 45 degree bevel of the roughing-out gouge, short as it is, must be applied so that it is at a rubbing angle, i.e. the handle of the tool is always lower than the cutting edge. Also, there is no need now to continue cutting just with the centre of the edge. *All* the edge can be used by twisting the gouge to either side, and a dig-in is almost impossible. I nearly wrote 'quite impossible', but I have only taught a few thousand pupils, and the next may be the one to do it. The main thing is to relax, reduce the grip on the gouge from what is sure to be a knuckle-whitening hold to the sort of gentle one we use when welcoming a lady.

Driving a car illustrates this too. When learning, the wheel is held far too tightly and the car can wander erratically all over the road, defeating all attempts to control it. A gouge, and especially the roughing-out gouge, is a tool made to do a specific job and will do it by itself if allowed. But a learner-turner can make hard work of it.

The lathe can be stopped at intervals to see if the wood has been turned down to a complete cylinder, but the professional way is to trail the tips of the fingers over the revolving wood, and any irregularity such as a slight remaining flat, is easily felt. Touch and hearing are senses useful for woodturning. After experience, some slight new sensation when turning with the gouge will be felt when it is dealing with say a knot in the wood. An indefinable 'clicking' noise denotes a split lengthwise in the grain, sometimes so fine that it is hard to see until searched for when the wood has been stopped. A sensation of slight judder coming through the handle probably means that the wood has slackened between the centres.

After the practice piece has been roughed down to a cylinder, the surface can be improved by using the roughing-out gouge on its side, utilising one half of its curved edge 'flat' (bevel rubbing) on the wood as though it was a chisel.

Once cutting has started, the edge of the tool is not looked at, the gaze being transferred to the top of the revolving wood, and the amount and area of cut is governed accordingly. A flat chisel used this way would be bound to dig in, but since the gouge is not flat, but curved, this does not happen and any irregularities in the roughed out surface can be smoothed away by traversing in either direction, and the final finish should be almost as good as that obtained with a trimming chisel.

An amateur way of obtaining a true cylinder, same diameter all along the length, is to rough down the wood, set calipers to the diameter required, and cut notches with the parting tool at intervals all along the wood, taking the notches down until the caliper legs just clear them. Then take down all surplus wood between the notches and the job is done.

Besides roughing down, both sizes of roughing gouges can be used for shallow curving and shaping. They are most useful tools, and the large sized spindle gouges with very shallow flutes that are sometimes used instead make poor substitutes.

The cylinder can now be practised on with the long and strong chisel, and then for cutting beads.

Using the Long and Strong Straight-Across Chisel

In the hands of an expert, all sorts of tricks can be demonstrated with a chisel, provided the right sort of wood is being used. It should be remembered that demonstration work need not necessarily be indicative of trade practice. For instance, if we wish to remove large quantities of timber, the roughing gouge will do a much quicker job than a chisel, and in business, time is money. An example of where a chisel is used to save time would be in the manufacture of large quantities of straight turned work, e.g. a tapered leg. This is shaped quickly and efficiently almost exactly to finished size with a few runs of the roughing gouge. The chisel is then brought into use for a quick 'planing' trim down the length of the leg, and the finish so obtained needs no time spent on papering. So we could regard the chisel as a finishing tool only.

A basic turnery rule is that wood is always cut from large diameter to small diameter, i.e. one is always going 'downhill'. This rule applies to the chisel. It is also not possible to start a cut with a chisel from the very end of the wood, since there is no support for the blade, and the edge can dig in and take out a chunk of timber. The cut can be started, say 1″ from the end of the wood, taken right to and off the other end, then the chisel is turned round and the remaining 1″ finished off the first end.

Cutting should take place from the TOP of the timber, i.e. the hand-rest is raised considerably more than considered necessary for other tool-work.

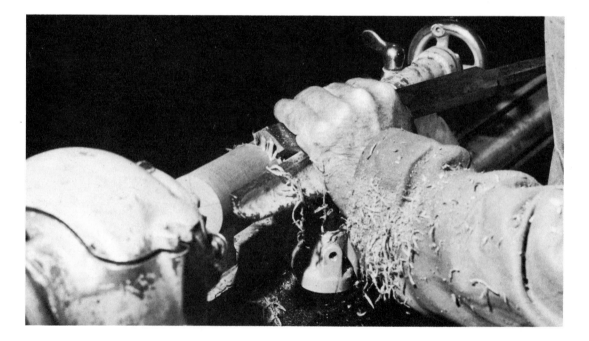

58a. Cutting with the long and strong square-across chisel. The hand-rest is brought up so that the action is on top of the work. The angle of cutting is a safe one as the right-hand corner of the chisel is farthest away from wood. The working stance is such that the long handle is held against the right side of the body for control and good support.

Some hand-rests will not go as high as they should, especially where large diameter work is being done. When large quantities of such turnings have to be made, it is usually found that the metal rest has been drilled and tapped for screws, and a wooden rest fitted to it to make a higher fence.

Like the bowl-turning gouge, it is the trailing point of a chisel that will dig in and cause damage if allowed to come into contact with the wood. The leading corner can be used to cut and will do so without any danger, but it is not good practice to use it always. Say 1/16″ from the leading point to within ⅛″ of the trailing point, and all or any of this length can cut without risk of dig-in. It is possible to cant the chisel to an angle so that the trailing point is at maximum clearance from the wood, and the chisel cuts small shavings with the centre of the edge. This is the starting position for the beginner. However, when practice brings more confidence and control, the *closer* the trailing point can be taken to the wood without actually touching it, the better, since the chisel is then at the best cutting angle of all and gives the wood a 'clean shave'.

Despite what you may read to the contrary, a skew chisel is not a substitute for a straight-across. If you try using a skew for these cutting

58b. Using chisel at its best angle, the 'dig-in' right corner just clearing the wood. This angle brings off a better shaving. The chisel is traversing from right to left.

angles, instead of a straight-across, the tool handle will have to be in an almost impossible position away from the body, and only comfortable when taking off the most meagre and unsatisfactory shaving from the very centre of the blade.

Cutting Beads

To practise these, the long and strong beading and parting tool (or a ¼″ square-across chisel as a substitute) is used, parting tool fashion, to cut notches into the cylinder at random intervals and varying depths. The rectangular sections between the notches are to be transformed into nicely rounded beads, some thick, some thin. It will help for uniformity on both sides of the bead, to run a pencil point at the middle of the bead-to-be, the idea being that whatever the final shape of bead, whether well rounded, or sharply peaked, the pencil line on the middle circumference, the equator, is to remain untouched by the tool. The basic principle in cutting is that when the bead is rounded to the right, then the right hand point of the tool always starts to cut and remains on the wood during all its travels round and down the side of the bead. To do this, the point is 'feathered' into the wood, i.e. the chisel is almost flat on the wood, the handle is twisted clockwise and brought upwards at the same time. The point must always be in contact with the wood, the rest of the chisel just follows round behind it. The point must always start the cut. It is useless to present the tool so that the blade is 'astride' the corner of the bead, thereby attempting to cut with the centre of the edge instead of the point. The tool, like the bowl-turning gouge, will only dig in with the trailing point, i.e. the point that is not doing the cutting. If the point that is doing the cutting is allowed to leave the wood, and this can happen more down at the bottom of the bead due to the fault that the handle is not being lifted up high enough, then the trailing point will almost certainly catch in wood and splinter it. Attempting to remove too much wood in one cut is another fault, since the cutting point can jib at too much work in one go, leaves the wood, and the trailing point then gets its chance for damage. The cutting point must not be allowed to come away from the wood that it is cutting until the cut is completed.

The beginner will not realise for some time how much he is unconsciously restricting the movement of the tool. The really tense (not dense) beginner will just manage to start a cut when unaccountably the edge leaves the wood. He finishes up with 'umpteen' ineffectual jabs. The chap with the more settled disposition manages a little better; the couldn't care less type either makes a complete hash of the whole operation, or does it beautifully first time. The secret is in the handle of the tool and not the

59a. Using a plain or long and strong parting tool. The point is pushed in at a scraping angle to enter the wood and start the cut. This scraping angle must be changed to a cutting one as soon as clean entry has been made.

59b. Entry has been made and now the handle of the parting tool is lowered so that the edge is working more on top of the wood and removing shavings at a cutting angle. Used this way, the cut is cleaner and the edge remains sharp.

59c. The end of a deep cut with the parting tool. The handle end is now much higher than the point so that the edge is still cutting on top of the wood. The cut has been slightly widened so that the tool does not bind and burn at the sides.

business end. When I was in troopships it was always the blunt end that did the driving and steered the sharp end in the right direction.

When cutting to the right, one way of holding the beading tool is to have it lying on the rest in a cutting angle position (bevel to rub, not edge to scrape), the thumb of the left hand on top of the blade and two fingers gripping it from underneath in a pincer fashion close to the rest. Assume this to be a pivot through which the blade will be turned. The right hand holds the handle at the extreme end in a hammer-grip, thumb on top or slightly to the left side. With the edge almost flat to the wood, the right hand point is entered at site of cut. Assume then that the wrist of the right hand holding the handle is mounted in a ball-race. The handle is therefore swivelled in this, the thumb coming up and over in a clockwise direction. In an accurately set up machine, this action must result in a perfectly executed half-circle cut, especially if a refinement is introduced that allows the 'ball-race' to rise vertically at the same time as the handle is swivelled.

The beginner just has to learn to do this swivelling action confidently without a trace of hesitation or interruption. There is no hurry about it. It can be just as well executed in slow motion; but it must be done smoothly. Any jerkiness in the handle movement, due almost entirely to nervousness and lack of confidence, will repeat like a needle gauge at the cutting end. Further study of the cutting end must show that the right action keeps the leading point in the wood where it should be, meanwhile continuously taking the trailing point out of harm's way.

60a. Start of the right-hand side of a bead, using the long and strong beading and parting tool. The blade is held at a cutting angle, the right-hand point has been feathered in to start cutting. The fingers and rest are being used as a pivot, the handle will be rolled round to the right and brought upwards as the cut proceeds. The right hand point must *not* be allowed to leave the wood once the cut has been started.

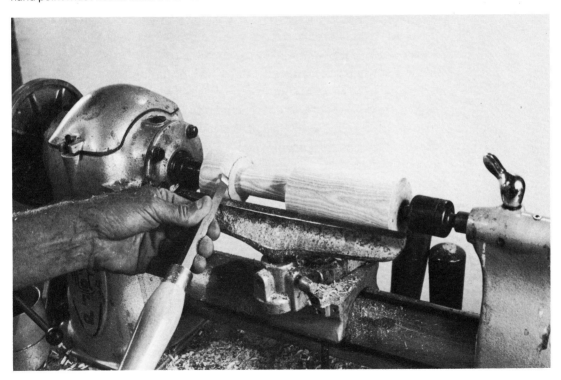

60b. Right-hand side of bead almost completed. The handle is coming up, the blade is being rolled over to the right, keeping the cutting point in timber, the trailing point clear. The handle will be higher than the point at completion of cut.

The rules for completing the left-hand side of the bead are the same. It is of advantage, if not so crucial as in bowl turning, to be able to reverse the hands and be ambidexterous, but let this be an exercise for the future, when more confidence has been established.

It is not to be expected that a beginner, however good at following written instructions, will get away without at least one dig-in, a flinching experience that tears out a chunk of wood from the bead-to-be, or deeply scars it. There can be more trouble if the beginner persists at the operation, because the tool, once led astray, can find the same drunken route at the next approach, and make the damage worse and worse. The speed of the revolving wood can hide the inflicted damage until the lathe is stopped, and then the beginner gets a shock when he sees what he has done to the inoffensive timber. In practice, it is far better for him to take up the roughing gouge again and smooth out the scars, then start again on a virgin surface.

Finally, like the chisel, the long and strong beading and parting tool must be sharpened *often* and the bevel kept hollow-ground or flat. It cannot be stressed too much that the biggest trouble a beginner can get into is caused by bluntness and brute force.

Skew Chisel for Cleaning up End Grain

When a notch is cut down into wood with a parting tool or beading and parting tool, the sides of the cut are raw and frayed out, since the sides of the tool are involved in a scraping action that unavoidably tears out fibres of wood to greater or lesser extent depending on the type of wood being turned. For example, the end grain of a piece of softwood, treated this way, is a pitiful sight. The remedy then is to *cut* a thin slice from the raw sides, using a long-cornered chisel to do so. This is a cleaning up operation. The chisel, keenly sharpened, is presented on the rest with the long-cornered point well up (handle held well down), and at a sideways angle to the wood so that a bevel is in line (parallel) with the side of the notch. The point is entered into the wood not more than 1/16″ away, i.e. the notch will be widened by that amount. The skimming cut is made by bringing up the handle of the chisel, using the fingers and rest as a pivot. The point of the chisel does the cutting, the bevel follows the point and since it is parallel to the sides of the notch, the bevel rubs wood as the point goes down in an arcing, slicing cut. A thin skim 1/16″ thick is removed and the remaining surface should be clean-cut and almost polished by the rubbing of the bevel. The point cuts the broken fibres to leave a clean surface. If the skew chisel is presented in such a fashion that the bevel does not rub and follow the point, two things can happen. The cut may come off well, but the result

61. Using the point of the long-cornered long and strong chisel to clean up end grain. The cut has been started with the point entering high up (handle well down—almost vertical). The cut is a slicing one, shown halfway through, the handle has been raised considerably and will end up higher than the point. The blade of the chisel is inclined to the right so that the left-hand bevel is following the point and is parallel to the cut so that the bevel rubs during the full duration of the cut. The left hand and rest are being used as a pivot.

will either by a curve, or at an angle which is not at right-angles to the cylinder. This can be done deliberately if this is the result required. Or the point can come off the wood that it is cutting, and a gash occurs. A gash or incompleted cut can also result if too thick a shaving is attempted. Using a skew chisel for a cleaning up operation depends for its success on the state of the point, which initiates the cut and does nearly all the work. The skew (long-cornered) point must be maintained at its original angle as when new, must be kept sharp, and sharpened carefully so that there is no suggestion of any rounding of the acute corner. The arcing (slicing action) of the cut is important. Some sort of result can be achieved by push-cutting the skew point into the wood without any pivoting action.

This is one of the finest ways of over-heating the point and getting a nice blue tinge on it.

Roy Child HSS Parting Tool

Made to a new design from high grade alloy steel, this is a great improvement over the conventional parting tool which, however skilfully used, rakes up the grain leaving a rough finish.

This tool has a pronged cutting edge which scribes the wood before it cuts. This gives the end grain a planed finish which in most cases needs no further work. It can be used directly on square section turnings without splintering the corners. This is very useful for pummels on furniture legs etc.

62. Roy Child high-speed steel parting tool.

The width of cut is only ⅛″ which saves a lot of wood in production work. Due to the exceptional quality of the steel the edge will remain sharp far longer than conventional tools, but when sharpening is needed it must be done correctly. To sharpen, grind the front face or bevel, taking care to maintain the original angle. Do not grind the flute on the *under* side of the tool as this is accurately shaped to give the prongs their clean cutting action. However, a careful rub inside the flute with a correctly shaped slipstone can be used to remove the burr.

It is important to use the tool the right way up with the flute *underneath*. The tool is used in an arching action, the handle being lifted progressively as the cut deepens. For deep cuts the operation should be done in stages with the cut being widened slightly at each stage to prevent binding. The steel will withstand the blueing due to friction in difficult timbers and will stay sharp even when used on hard and abrasive tropical woods.

Use of the Long-cornered (Skew) Chisel for Leaving Squares, or Pummels

This is usually needed when turning legs for chairs or tables, and some portion of the wood has to be left untouched and square so that they can be morticed in the normal way, and rails tenoned into them. These untouched portions are also termed pummels. An example would be a set of four short legs, made out of 2″ × 2″ stock, for a rectangular topped Jacobean style stool.

When a sawn size of wood is planed, its measurements then become 'nominal' instead of actual, so that planed 2″ × 2″ stock is really in the region of 1⅞″ × 1⅞″.

It is of advantage for a turner doing work of this nature to use sawn, not planed, stock. The reason will be given later. The legs are squared all round at the points where the ends of the square (untouched wood) and the rest of the leg (turned down to a cylinder), intersect. This is done on the bench with tri-square and heavy soft pencil, so that the lines can still be seen when the wood is revolving in the lathe. The ends of the wood are centred in the usual way, taking care that the wood will run true. The leg is then mounted in the lathe and the rest adjusted so that when the wood is turned round by hand, the corners just clear the edge of the rest. When the lathe is started, these revolving corners make a distinct shadow (see roughing down) and the pencilled lines can also be seen distinctly. The skew chisel is put on the rest with the long-cornered point upwards (handle well down) so that when the handle is brought up the point goes down into the corners of the wood in a slicing arc. The object first is to form a V notch with small cuts alternately each side of the marked pencil line, similar to felling a tree with a timber axe. When in the right position to use the chisel for this purpose, the shadow of the revolving corners cannot be seen, and have to be 'felt' for with the point of the chisel. It will surprise most people

63a. Leaving squares. Wood marked and mounted in the lathe, corners clearing rest.

63b. Leaving squares. Camera has 'stopped' wood in revolution, but clearly shows shadows of corners.

63c. Leaving squares. Wood at turning speed, marked ends of squares clearly visible. Shadow of revolving corners.

63d. Leaving squares. The long corner of the chisel is used to cut into the revolving corners. The handle is coming up as the cut is deepened. The camera has stopped the action at a point where the chisel is not cutting, but the top corner will have a further chip removed when it reaches the blade.

how far it is away from what seems to be solid revolving wood that the point first makes contact. As soon as a small V cut has been started, it is widened and deepened, by further slicing cuts each side, but in order to make clean cutting slices at each stroke, it is important that only thin shavings should be attempted, and also that the bevel follows the point. This means that in deepening the V from the right, the point is entered to start the cut, and the blade of the chisel inclined over to the right so that the side of the bevel follows down behind the cut and rubs the side of the V. Failure to do this will cause the point to jump about in uncontrolled fashion and instead of cutting clean causes a mass of gashes.

Cutting is complete when the point of the enlarged V meets all round the square. After some experience, this can be judged to a nicety without stopping the lathe, by watching the shadow at this point gradually disappearing, but the beginner had better stop the lathe to see how things are progressing.

Cleaning Up

Feeling for the corners of revolving wood can be a little 'hit-or-miss', and it is quite easy to make a false start and give the corners some undesirable

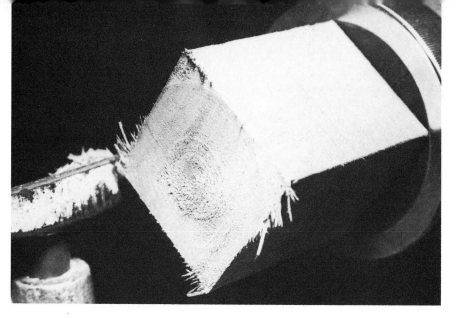

64a. The ragged result of using a plain parting tool to cut into a square (e.g. making a pummel).

64b. The almost planed finish from the pronged cutting tip of the new parting tool, with minimum or no damage to the corners of the square.

small gashes. If sawn wood has been used, the sides of the squares can be planed down after turnery has been completed, so removing the blemishes and reducing the size of the squares to the nominal $1\frac{7}{8}'' \times 1\frac{7}{8}''$. If planed wood is started with, then much more care will be needed when cutting squares or pummels.

Cutting a Right-angle Pummel

The V method of cutting leaves a square with rounded corners; sometimes for a design it is necessary to leave these corners sharply right-angled, and

65. Turning an ogee pummel with a gouge. Gouge has been entered on its side flute facing left, and is being turned over on its back to complete the cut.

the method here is to line up the bevel of the skew chisel at right angles to the wood so that the first cut is straight-in and not at an angle. The second cut angles in from the side, the next straight-in, and so on, so that the completed cut is half a V.

It must be remembered that in all these cuts with the long corner, the point is brought down into the wood in a slicing arc action, never pushed directly in. Doing the latter will sooner or later overheat and damage the point. The Roy Child Parting Tool can easily and successfully be used for perfect simple pommels in lieu of the more difficult skew chisel.

Cutting Ogee Pummels with a Gouge
A square can have its ends left with a decorative double curve known as ogee. This is fashioned by cutting with a spindle gouge of about ½″. The method of cutting is the same as described for general use of this gouge i.e., treat the square of wood as a cylinder. The gouge is entered on its side, the point 'feeling' for the corners of the wood, and then scooped over so that it finishes on its back, flute uppermost. Only a chip or two is removed at first, then the gouge is started at the other side and brought back to the centre. The slight hollow thus formed is gradually deepened this way, cutting alternately from sides to middle, until the centre of the hollow is of completely rounded wood.

Removing Waste Wood between Squares
This is done with the roughing down gouge. Assume that a square has been left at either end of the wood, the waste between to be removed until

66a. The squares completed. Waste between to be removed.

66b. Removing waste between squares. The roughing out gouge has started a cut with the extreme left-hand corner, gouge completely on its side.

66c. Removing waste between squares. The roughing out gouge has traversed the waste from left to right, being rolled over at the same time and ending up completing the cut with the extreme right-hand corner.

66d. Waste completely removed between squares. The next stage is to incorporate any turning detail that may be required.

it is a cylinder.

The roughing down gouge is presented to the side of the square on the left, completely on its side with the flute facing left. It is pushed in so that the bottom corner (left-hand corner) starts cutting, and the cutting continued by rolling the gouge clockwise, cutting all the time with some part of its edge. The waste wood is traversed to the right, and the gouge finishes up at the side of the right-hand square, completely rolled over so that it is now on its other side, flute facing right and cutting with the bottom corner, the right-hand corner.

The gouge does a complete 180 degree turn, rolling along the rest. Using it this way will remove waste right up to the sides of the squares, the cylinder that has been made between them can now be beaded, grooved, or otherwise shaped to requirements.

Cutting Hollows with a Spindle Gouge

A gouge, when presented to the wood, is held on its side, the flute facing in the direction of the hollow to be scooped out. It is at the moment of penetration that the gouge is most likely to misbehave and kick sideways. This is because the cutting edge has nothing to support it at first, and it

67a. Cutting a hollow with a spindle gouge. The point is entered with the gouge on its side, and firmness is needed to prevent it slipping side-ways to left before it has entered enough so that it forms its own fence. Angling the handle to the right can help at this 'precise point of entry' stage.

67b. Finish of cut doing left-hand side of hollow with spindle cutting gouge. The blade, held on its side on entry, has now been brought over completely on its back, the cut being a scooping action with the bevel always resting on wood. In this final position, the action must not be continued much beyond centre of hollow, otherwise it will start cutting uphill, which is incorrect. The other side of the hollow is done the other way.

needs firm guidance from its master to tell it in what direction to proceed. It won't do it any good to inform it verbally where it can consign itself, however great the provocation.

'Precise point of entry' crops up again, as in bowl turning. An example is indicated. There is a left and right hand side to a hollow. Starting at the left, the gouge is held on the hand-rest, on its side, at right angles to the wood and horizontal, the flute pointing to the right. The point of the nose just rubs the wood at the required place of entry. It is firmly and slowly pushed into the wood until it has just entered. When this has happened, the gouge cannot then slip sideways to the left because the wood supports the bevel and stops it, acting as a fence. If the gouge, instead of being presented exactly at right angles to the wood, is slightly angled, i.e. the handle more to the right, this can be a help in preventing any sideways slip.

The hollowing from the left is started with a scooping action, the fingers holding the blade on the rest acting as a pivot and the hand holding the handle twisting it round in an *anti*-clockwise rotation.

The gouge cannot turn properly 'uphill', so a hollow is formed with alternate scoops from each side to the centre, until it is of the required depth and shape. At the start of the hollowing out cuts, the gouge starts always on its side, but always ends up at the centre of the hollow, on its back, so in fact it goes downhill and rolls backward at the same time. This ensures that the wood is cut with the bevel always rubbing, and not just scraped out with only the edge of the gouge.

Avoiding Ribbing

Ribbing, a kind of coarse screw-thread effect that spoils what should be a smooth turned surface, can be due to several causes, and the serious enthusiast should begin by eradicating those that are well within his control, e.g. poor tools, toolwork, lathe and accessory defects.

The lathe should be checked for steadiness, and to make sure all the pulleys are running smoothly and correctly (see page 19).

Lathe centres should be kept in good condition, the driving centre sharp. The tail centre is for support only, and should not be screwed up to hold the wood excessively tight between centres.

A heavy long and strong chisel is easiest to control as its weight helps to keep it in place and damps down vibration better than the ligher versions. It is essential that it is kept extremely sharp, with no rounding of the bevels. Under perfect conditions, it is still possible to cause ribbing with the chisel, and then the only remedy is to do the required work as well as possible with a gouge, a much easier tool than the chisel for working on thin diameters.

A 10″ length of beech, ash, pine, or similar straight grained wood, 2″ in diameter, should come down to 1″ in diameter without any trace of ribbing, using a chisel. If ribbing does occur, and the lathe and tools, etc. have all been checked, then the beginner is just not using his chisel properly and the only cure is more practice. It will not be of much use trying out the following aids otherwise.

Slender diameter wood can be pushed out of true rotation by just the cutting pressure of the chisel, and then ribbing is bound to occur. This can be controlled by using one hand behind the work, thumb on top of the chisel blade, and pulling the wood towards the user, thereby cancelling out the opposite chisel pressure, and keeping the wood running true. This can also be helpful when using a gouge in similar circumstances. Wearing a glove might be of help to sensitive flesh not used to such artisan treatment. Horny-handed turners have callouses in all sorts of odd places.

Mechanical Steadies

Since wood in a lathe is only held at the two ends, and has no support, such as a bench, underneath it, it is fairly obvious that in the case of a long length of thin diameter, there can occur considerable whip in the middle, and some kind of support here can help to control it. The oldest form of mechanical steady was made of wood. A stand to be clamped to the bed of the lathe, and to take a length of wood, pivoted to the stand at the bottom and with a V notch at the top of it that bears on the revolving wood from the back. The pivot piece with notch is kept to its work by a top-weighted wedge slid between it and the back of the stand.

Where rectangular stock is being turned, it is first roughed down with a gouge to a round at the central point so that the V notch of the steady can

68. Using fingers to steady slender work, thumb holding down chisel.

69. Wooden steady in use.

engage on it from behind. It has to be in close contact with the turning wood, in fact it should tend to force the wood slightly out of true revolution towards the turner so that this can be corrected by the pressure of the tool against it. Friction will soon make V notch and wood blacken, char and smoke. I have never had it actually burst into flames yet.

The required turning is finished from headstock to steady, and from the other side of the steady to the tail centre. The steady is then removed and the short charred remainder of the turnery gently dealt with; usually using a small sharp gouge as the finishing tool.

A mechanical steady has been developed, where the V notch is formed by the space between two mounted revolving castor wheels. These bear against the top and bottom of the revolving wood from the back, and in theory dispose of the burning friction that occurs between wood and wood. However it may not perform as well as the cruder wood version, since there had to be some play in the castor bearings or they would not revolve. This play could be transmitted to the wood, which is just what a steady should prevent.

Use of Scraper Tools between Centres on Spindle Work

Advice on this might be difficult. Some books on woodturning that I have read mention such cutting tools as gouge and chisels in such a cursory manner that they seem to have been included only because it is known that they exist. Description of their use is hedged around with nervous 'watch it, be careful, could be dangerous' cautionary detail, and then, what is much worse, the reader is firmly guided to the safer merits of scraping tools, so that he may well believe that using sharp cutting tools in woodturnery is mere professional exhibitionism, and that exactly similar results can be achieved by scraping. I can quite firmly denounce this as untrue, but yet am unable to prohibit entirely the use of scrapers on spindle work. There are occasions when it is essential to use one; an example would be on a surface that slopes up to terminate sharply against the shoulder of a beaded detail. A chisel cannot be used, since it would be working 'uphill', and this is against a basic principle in turnery, and it cannot work from the other direction because the bead is in the way. It is handy to have a wide straight scraper to use lightly for truing up the finish of a cylinder to fine limits, but to use a scraper to form a plain bead, after all the close instruction that has been given on the use of a long and strong beading and parting tool, this is cowardice. I'll leave it to individual consciences.

Turn the odd piece of pine to a cylinder between centres and give it a planed finish with the sharp square-edge chisel. Then with a scraper try to scrape the surface smoother. If you succeed, write a book about it!

11. Two Multi-Purpose Chucks

It is almost essential to have some device capable of holding wood of any dimension so securely at the headstock end of the lathe that there is no need whatsoever for any support by the tailstock end, so that one end is completely accessible, e.g. for drilling or hollowing out. This enables the turner to work on the wood safely and unencumbered. Secureness is especially important where end-grain is involved, i.e. where the grain of the wood is lengthways along the lathe bed. Screws do not hold safely enough in end-grain, unless they are so long and large that valuable timber is sacrificed in waste.

There are a variety of chucks on the market designed for this purpose, but these have been found to be unsatisfactory in that they either limit the size of wood that can be used in them, or are not reliable in their hold. For instance, the three- or four-jawed chuck, so helpful in metal turning, can be dangerous when used for wood. If the jaws are tightened gently enough not to bruise the wood, they can give up their hold at some stage of the turning process. If they are tightened too much, they not only crush the timber but also throw it out of centre.

My son Roy, after some years of experimenting and improving, has patented the Child Coil Grip Chuck, which will meet the most exacting demands of the woodturner, experienced or not. This new invention is made for most makes of lathe, and he is now supplying them to customers both at home and abroad.

The chuck, with its attachments, can be used to hold work securely by numerous methods. It will handle all sizes of timber, from a lace-needle to the biggest piece the lathe can take, all without need of tailstock support. To give some idea of its versatility, a short description follows.

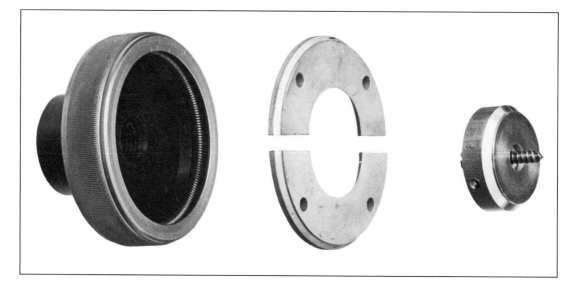

70. The Roy Child coil grip chuck showing coil grip assembly, split reducing ring and screwchuck adaptor.

First, the main body is drilled to take screws and act as a small faceplate. There is also a central coarse-thread hole, and this holds the work if a short stub-end is first turned on it. The wood is then screwed into the centre hole and provides an amazingly firm grip. An outside ring fits on to the main body that is threaded and can take wood of 3½″ diameter or less, length immaterial. A split metal washer is held by the ring and body and will take wood 2½″ × 2½″ square, a notch is cut near the end of the wood and the two halves of washer (or split ring) fitted round it. A wood screw and metal fitting is also provided that can be used to convert it to a screw chuck.

A brand new patented idea makes the chuck even more versatile. Many so-called universal chucks are about, but their limiting factor is that the wood must not be too big to fit through the main ring. There is a collet variety which works by expansion, but too much force can cause damage. A coil grip works by the much safer method of *compression*, and this is achieved by means of a simple length of coil spring fitted into the main ring, which is specially machined to take it. The wood to be turned is taken down at one end to a flange which is then held by the spring, and when tightened exerts an even force from each of the hundreds of small coils all round the wood. In addition, since the wood can be offered up to the chuck from outside, i.e. not *through* the ring, there is no limit to diameter or length of timber—if your lathe can take it, so can the chuck! Finally, the

71. The steel dovetail-shaped ring is pushed forward by the front plate being drawn towards the rear by tightening four nuts at the back of the chuck. The ring then expands to fit the recess in the wood and the gap in the ring closes up, giving enormous equal holding power all around the recess.

72. A huge bowl safely held by the ring chuck which holds the wood close to the headstock and so greatly helps the bearings to take the load.

turner can make his own wooden chucks and fittings for any special job, e.g. his own reducing rings, and these can be accurately used time and time again since the chuck automatically accepts and centres them.

For the outboard or rear turning end of the lathe, Roy has produced his Bowl Chuck, which works by an expanding mechanism which locks into a dovetail shaped recess, and can safely hold the heaviest disc of timber without any need of screws, so great big bowls can be turned, or the shallowest of platters. Both chucks are very strong, but amazingly gentle in that they do not mar the wood in any way, or damage polished work.

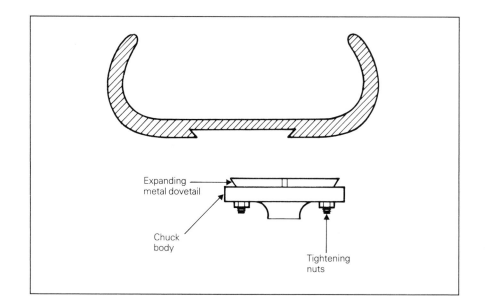

73. Diagram of the bowl chuck.

12. Safety in the Workshop

Schools and factories have the benefit of the experience and advice of inspectors and safety officers who issue written regulations regarding safety precautions. Modern lathes and accompanying machines are well equipped with 'fail-safe' switches that will stop them if any attempt is made to use them unguarded, and therefore unsafely. If you are woodturning as a commercial business, or if you are employing anyone in your workshop there are Government regulations on safety with which you must comply.

Being self-taught I learned the craft of woodturning the hard way, and this included the knowledge of how to avoid injury. It is just unfortunate that, before these lessons were learned, the injuries had to happen!

The Lathe

When wood is fixed to the lathe and the rest adjusted for work on it, it is wise, before switching on, to turn over the wood by hand *several* times to ensure that the rest or some other part of the lathe is not interfering with the swing of the wood. The levers and wingnuts that secure the rest in position should be checked for tightness. Fortunately, if the rest is not checked or for any reason gets into the path of the revolving wood, it usually acts as a guard itself and throws the timber away from the operator, or if not, at least tends to reduce the impact.

This is comforting for the operator, but may not be so for any spectator, who may be standing in the direct path of the projectile. In this instance, it is the *watcher* who is most at risk. The safest place for the spectator, just before the lathe is switched on, is *behind* the operator.

74. Sturdy little lathe made in a school craftroom: for turning between centres. Photograph Mr Ian Crookes.

Any woodturning tool should be in contact with the rest *before* it touches the revolving wood. Failure to do this can result in pinched and lacerated fingers and a possible facial injury from a flying splinter.

I suppose that the ultimate in safety would be for the turner to wear gloves, goggles, and facemask, but I cannot see many enthusiasts enjoying their work encumbered so. Specks of wood in unprotected eyes is a common happening, and the turner can choose to wear glasses, or if not, experience soon teaches him when working, how to hold his head to avoid them.

I have already discussed the danger of using thin files as scrapers, but will again stress the importance of employing any scraping tool in a trailing approach to the wood, i.e. the handle of the tool is always held higher than the cutting edge, so that any dig-in will force the edge downwards and out of the wood, rather than up and further into it.

Sanding on the lathe has usually more irritating results than harmful ones, although prolonged sanding of 'dusty' woods such as mahogany or iroko, cannot be good for 'the tubes'. A nurse's cheap lint mask, or even a handkerchief over the nose and mouth, is a good idea. When sanding the inside of a large bowl, the paper is safest used in a position where the wood is descending down on to it. To explain, stand in front of the inside of the revolving bowl. If it is revolving clockwise, the lower right hand quadrant is the safest area on which to hold the paper. For better pressure and quicker results, I push the paper all around the inside of the bowl, and have forgotten now how often my fingers were bent back with very painful results until I learned to control them. All my knuckles are now of the double-jointed variety.

The Grindstone

Well-guarded stones, such as found installed in metalwork shops, have close-fitting top caps, flat table tool supports, and a transparent vizor, as additional protection against sparks. Face goggles should be regarded as essential.

The stone should not be run at an excessive speed, and the manufacturer usually has a note to this effect on a new stone, giving the maximum tested r.p.m. as a reference. The stone, when away from its power source and therefore not fitted, should be handled as carefully as if it was made of glass, and when tapped with a tool handle or similar implement, should 'ring' like a bell to prove that it is not cracked. There should be packing pieces, e.g. cardboard discs, between the metal clamping cheeks that squeeze the stone and hold it securely on its arbor, and the securing nut should not be over tightened. The stone should revolve towards the user, not away from him. Sparks from the metal tool are then deflected downwards and not up into his face.

The surface of the stone should be clean and not glazed, i.e. a shiny surface indicating that the grit particles are blunted and the spaces in between full of waste metal. Grindstone dressing tools are available for cleaning and also straightening worn stones.

Provided that the stone is of the right grit specification, clean and in good condition, then only the very minimum of pressure is required for grinding and sharpening tools quickly and efficiently without overheating and destroying their temper (and yours).

The Bandsaw

This is another essential machine for the enthusiast turner who wants speed and efficiency in his work. They differ in size from the huge monsters in sawmills to small models capable of cutting out intricate jigsaw puzzles. Machines with three supporting wheels round which the endless saw-blade runs provide a wider throat for material than two-wheel types where the throat is restricted to the diameter of the wheel used. The two-wheeler can be cheaper, easier to adjust and not so demanding on the flexibility of the saw-blade, so since the turner has little need for cutting wide pieces of wood, this is the machine recommended for him. If a machine is capable of cutting wood up to say 6″ thickness, it will therefore handle 3″ and 4″ stuff without strain or effort, so the more powerful machine provides the better safety factor. Saw-blades come in various widths and ⅜″ wide will be found the most useful size for cutting wood into discs to a turner's requirements. A ¼″ blade can be a little on the fragile side, and ½″ might create difficulty in small diameter work.

If commonsense precautions are taken, they are very safe machines in use. The manufacturer supplies instructions for the fitting and tensioning of the blade. The depth guide and *guard* should be adjusted so that the thickness of wood passes underneath with only a slight clearance. A blunt blade means excessive pressure on the wood to make it cut.

Since a woodturner is often cutting thicker wood than is, say, a cabinet-maker, the woodcutting sawblades supplied do not last long without the need for sharpening. I found this a tedious process, so a manufacturer makes my blades from metal-cutting hardened steel, but still with teeth most suitable for cutting wood. In addition, to lessen the friction of deep cutting, and cutting wet unseasoned wood, every alternate tooth is removed (skip-tooth blade). These blades last much longer than plain wood-cutting ones and can also be used, with suitable jigs, to cut copper and brass tubes into tool ferrule lengths.

The Hand-Rest

It occasionally becomes necessary to adjust the height of this to allow a different tool to be used. The safest way by far is to stop the lathe before doing this. If when satisfied by experience that you know the dangers and can still do this safely with the lathe running, I would not consider this unforgivable, but do not do it with a tool held in the hand *as well*.

PART II

PRACTICAL EXAMPLES

13. Handles for Long and Strong Tools

These should be longer and stouter than most factory-made equivalents, and although 1¾″ × 1¾″ sawn stock can be used, a more comfortable margin is given by the use of 2″ × 2″. A length of 13″ is needed. Suitable woods can be beech, ash, sycamore, box (expensive), teak, afrormosia, almost any hard wood that is close grained. This handle will suit all sizes of long and strong bowl turning gouges from ½″ to ¾″. Similar ones, made for heavy scrapers and the large size roughing-out gouges and long and strong chisels, can be 1″ or so shorter, a trifle thicker, and will need a larger ferrule, say ⅞″ or 1″ diameter.

Ferrule

Brass-cased tubing is not very strong and the thin brass covering can soon flake off. Solid drawn brass tube is not easy to obtain and is expensive. Copper tubing is also expensive but there may be a friendly plumber who can provide short ends from his working stock, and 1″ is long enough for a ferrule. ¾″ diameter is used for this handle. The ends are cut 'square' with a hacksaw, the inside rag removed with a round file or home-made cleaning tool, and the outside edges smoothed. The ferrule is slipped over the barrel of the tailstock, and a small dead ring or cone centre used. A revolving centre, because of its bulk, is not suitable.

The Handle

The wood is mounted in the lathe and turned down to a cylinder, using a roughing-down gouge. The end nearest the tailstock is then turned down a bare 1″ in length to a dowel that will be a tight fit into the ferrule. This is worked with a parting tool or long and strong beading and parting tool.

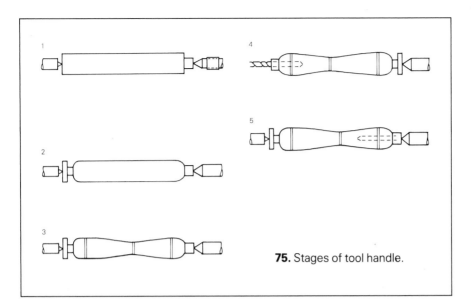

75. Stages of tool handle.

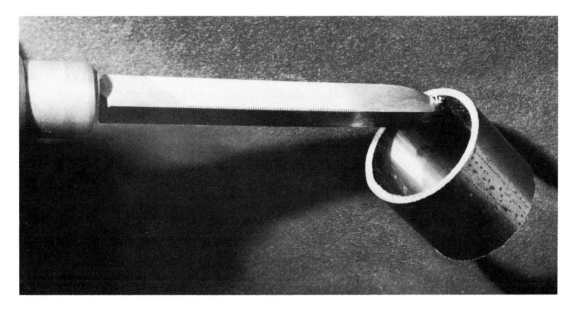

76. Cleaning the burr from the inside of a ferrule. The tool is made from an old triangular file, serrations ground off at the end and curve-bevelled to a point. The curved surfaces are oilstoned to produce three sharp cutting edges, any of which can be used.

The ferrule, already on the barrel, is used at intervals to test this diameter. Calipers could be set and used instead, but the former is the quicker method. A refinement is to form a small hollow at the base of the dowel (using point of small skew chisel), so that the ferrule end can be buried into it. Then the handle is taken off the lathe to do this, and a drift used as a driver. The drift can be another piece of copper tube, or a short piece of galvanised pipe of the same diameter. This is stronger material and will stand up to mallet blows.

Until experience is gained, it is quite easy to take too much off the dowel when turning it down, so that the ferrule does not fit tightly enough. To remedy this, a tap with a centre punch on two sides of the ferrule will 'pop' it and serve to hold it firmly. The handle is then replaced on the lathe.

About ½″ of waste is left at the driving end, then a ½″ wide notch cut into the wood to a depth where sufficient material is left to maintain the drive. ⅜″ diameter should be ample. This end of the handle is then rounded over, using the beading tool, and the end at the base of the ferrule given similar treatment. The handle is then shaped to a favoured design, using the ¾″ roughing out gouge. The traditional lines can be inscribed with the point of a small skew chisel.

A sheet of No. 2/0 (100 Grit) open coated garnet paper is folded in half lengthwise and held underneath the handle, both hands over the top and at either side of the handle, so the length of paper is held as a sling. This way, the handle can be quickly sanded, and any small irregularities left by the gouge, satisfactorily smoothed to a continuous contour more efficiently than if given individual attention with a small pad of paper. A second sanding follows with No. 4/0 (150 Grit) folded smaller, not forgetting to burnish up the copper ferrule.

After this, the perfectionist will stop the lathe, and sand the handle in line with the grain in order to get rid of circular scratches.

Polishing

With the lathe stopped, sanding sealer is applied to the handle with a rag, and rubbed well and firmly in. Put on quite enough to satisfy the pores of the wood. The drying process can be speeded up if the lathe is then started and the handle rubbed firmly with the rag. The precaution should be taken to fold all ends of the rag away into a neat pad so that no loose fibres can catch in the lathe centres. Final drying is ensured by rubbing with a handful of shavings. Quite an acceptable finish can be obtained with the use of sanding sealer alone, but it can be vastly improved by a good white friction polish. (The brown variety is not so suitable.) To do this, the lathe is started again, and the handle sanded with No. 9/0 (320) Grit, a very fine 'flour' paper. If the coat of sanding sealer is really dry, this will result in a cloud of white dust coming off the wood (the powder content of the sealer), and afterwards the handle should feel as smooth to the touch as a piece of silk.

Friction Polish

A few drops of friction polish are applied to a small pad of cotton wool (in U.S.A.—'batting'), and the handle, lathe stopped, is given a rubbed coat of the polish with this, spreading it thinly and evenly all over the surface. When engaged in spindle turning I screw a faceplate to the lefthand side of the headstock and use it to revolve the work by hand, in the same way as the housewife deals with her sewing machine. The lathe is started again and the handle rubbed with the cotton wool, gently at first, then increasing up to firm pressure as the shine grows. To ensure a good job, the cotton wool is used until it is absolutely dry. This is one reason why very little of the liquid friction polish is applied in the first instance, because otherwise working to a dry finish can be a tedious operation, and an excessive amount of polish can form ugly rings on the surface of the wood.

Properly and economically applied, friction polish gives a lasting shine to work of small diameter. Our perfectionist can now step in, and as an ultra-finishing touch run a block of wax lightly over the wood and burnish with a soft cloth.

Drilling for the Tang

The lathe is adjusted to run at its lowest speed, and a $5/16''$ or $3/8''$ drill inserted in the headstock. Engineers' drills with morse taper ends can be obtained, and these are very useful for drilling work in the lathe. Or a Jacob's chuck, also fitted with a morse taper end is an alternative, so that standard engineers' drills can be fitted into the chuck.

The ferrule end of the handle is brought up to the drill point, the end with the waste at the tail centre, the handle is held stationary by the left hand while the tail centre is screwed up with the right hand. The lathe is started and the hole for the tang drilled at least $2''$ deep by gradually screwing up the tail centre. The handle should be brought out from the drill at intervals so that waste wood can escape. Failure to do this could cause the drill to bind in the hole and wrench the handle round in the hand. There will not be any damage to flesh if this happens, but the polish could suffer!

Parting Off

The simplest and crudest method is to remove the handle from the lathe and saw off the waste with a tenon saw. The cut end then has to be sanded and finished by hand. The beginner can improve on this method, in that he can completely part off the handle with a parting tool while it it still revolving in the lathe. After the tang hole has been drilled, the handle is replaced in the lathe in its original position, a cone centre used to run in and support the hole at the ferrule end. In the absence of a cone or revolving centre, the tang hole can be plugged temporarily with dowel so that the standard ring centre can then be used instead—we try our best to cover all eventualities!

The secret of complete parting off is not to have the handle held too tightly between the centres. It should be just tight enough to drive, and no more. With the lathe running at turning speed, the 3⁄8″ dowel of the waste is gently thinned down with a sharp parting tool, the edge always working on top of the wood at a cutting angle, and moved sideways so that there is always ample clearance for the width of the blade. Gently does it, and the waste can be brought down easily to 1⁄8″ diameter without breaking through. The final stage is to operate the parting tool with one hand, the other one poised round but *not* holding the handle, and the nibbling continued until the moment of truth when the handle is completely separated from the driving waste. It may just possibly give a very slight kick but will then repose gently in the guarding hand, while the waste still revolves merrily away.

The perfectionist moves in again at the stage where the parting tool reaches the 1⁄8″ diameter, and repeats the instructions that followed, but

77. Final parting off of chisel handle. Small skew chisel, point used downwards, small slicing cuts in V shape. Guarding hand ready to catch handle when completely cut off and stops revolving.

replaces the parting tool with a keen ½″ skew chisel, using the point to enter the dowel right where it is attached to the handle. A slicing arc 'nick', followed by another to form a V, and so on until the dowel is cut neatly through at the handle end and the result is the same as that obtained by the parting tool, but a much cleaner finish.

This parting off operation, done by a professional with the dexterity and speed born of long experience, can look like magic to an awed beginner, but it is absurdly simple. After all, once the wood has been separated from its driving portion, there is nothing left to keep it moving, so it must almost immediately become inert and harmless. Brute force could possibly cause it to react a little more violently as it comes away, but we have no use for brute force in this craft.

A beautifully clean face can be obtained by first taking down the excess to approximately ¼″ diameter with a parting tool or beading and parting tool, then skimming the base with the Roy Child Parting Tool, which cleans up the end grain as the more awkward skew chisel would do. Complete the parting-off with the small skew chisel.

Fixing the Handle of the Tool

At school I had to learn about a basic principle that dealt with a force having an equal and opposite reaction. I now realise that I have been using this knowledge as a means of attaching handles to tools. The handle is held upright on the bench where a leg is directly underneath. The tang of the tool is dropped into the hole and the handle bounced up and down on the bench, so that the tang is gradually driven down and at the same time makes the hole fit its rectangular section. The wood directly around the tang sometimes splits, but it does not really matter, as the copper ferrule takes the strain easily. A habit that is worth while forming is to give the handle of a tool another bounce on the bench whenever it is picked up for use. If for any reason you are chary about taking my word for all this, just try to get the handle out again!

A good friend and master-turner used to demonstrate at exhibitions with a handle on his chisel that was a disgrace to his craft. He occasionally mentioned to his audiences that if he knew of a woodturner he would get a new one made, to take the place of what looked like a splintered piece of firewood bound round with copper wire and a bootlace. I took him at his word, and for a Christmas present made him a beautiful handle, decorated by my wife with her pyrographic art, and polished to perfection. He was duly appreciative, but I know for a fact that my magnificent handle reposes amongst trophies and curiosities in his home, while the offending one is still in its usual place. I've often wondered.

78. Mexican Palisandra goblet, massive afrormosia goblet with apple egg, normal egg-cup of Mango Machang with tulipwood egg.

14. Goblets and Egg Cups

The chosen wood for the goblet was Mexican Palisandra and beautifully marked. Starting dimensions 11″ × 4″ × 4″. The block was placed between centres, brought down to maximum cylinder size with a roughing down gouge, and then with gouge and calipers cut down carefully at the tailstock end so that one of the holding methods of the coil grip chuck could be employed. (See the egg cup example, photographs 79 and 80). The main ring of the chuck is hung over the tailstock ready for testing the final diameter of the cylinder.

79. Egg cup blank diameter being tested for close fit in metal flange ring.

To make sure of maximum support from the chuck backplate, the end of the cylinder was squared with the parting tool, any small projection left at the centre taken down so that it would fit easily into the backplate hole and therefore not obstruct the fit of the wood base. This is then held by the main ring screwed up to the body of the chuck.

Hollowing Out

This can be effected by a combination of different methods, but a basic principle affects them all. When boring or hollowing out wood, it is advisable to accomplish this if possible before doing any shaping work on the outside of the project, thereby having maximum thickness of wood around the hole so as to avoid any possibility of the tool used splintering out the thin sides.

With the hand-rest placed across and close to the face, most of the hollow can be formed with a ⅜″ long and strong deep fluted gouge with a pointed nose, entering it on its side, flute facing away, and rolled in cutting to the centre, handle twisted clockwise and lifting up as the edge approaches the centre of the hollow. This is quick, but fairly difficult at first. If the point keeps skidding at first contact, scrape a preliminary start with a parting tool.

80. Hollowing out egg cup. Scraper pointing down to centre of hollow, most of the cutting done from bottom outwards to keep with grain.

The hollow can be commenced by putting a drill in the tailstock and drilling to depth. Handy when sets of cups are being made, as then the drill can be marked to bore the same depth each time, and the final hollowing out, done with a rounded scraper, is stopped just as the marks of the drill point are reached and taken out. All hollows will then be the same depth.

Using a Rounded Scraper

Since the cutting edge of the tool has to point slightly downwards in use, the height of the rest across the face of the work must be adjusted accordingly. A difference of a mere 1/16″ in height can make a great deal of difference between smooth working of the scraper or a harsh judder, so the beginner should do some experimenting.

Paradoxically, the hollow is best scraped from the bottom outwards since this action comes with the grain, and should be remembered when doing the final smoothing cuts. The scraper needs a fair amount of push-pressure at the bottom of the hollow, but as soon as it commences to cut, the pressure is eased and the scraper handle taken well over to the other side when coming out at the lip. In other words, the handle swings in a large arc, otherwise it will be found that the hollow is not deep enough, and this can look wrong and amateurish. When finished to satisfaction the hollow is sanded and the rest adjusted parallel for work on the side.

Remembering that enough waste has to be left for parting off, a preliminary notch is cut with a parting tool near the chuck or base of the goblet. The hollow should also be measured and its depth shown by a pencil line on the outside. This is a guide when shaping, otherwise it is quite possible suddenly to find oneself with an odd-looking bracelet.

There is a choice of tools to use for shaping, a chisel, or a 1/2″ pointed nose spindle gouge. I prefer the latter because it is handier for quick curves, and almost as smooth cutting—if it is sharp!

Any curving required towards the lip of the cup should be tackled first, working, as always, from large to small diameter. If it is remembered that the cutting action of any tool involves the *lifting* of the handle, and never the reverse, this should help. Leave the wood at the base alone for the time being, because if any of this is cut away beforehand it can leave insufficient support for any toolwork at the rim end and can lead to a lot of trouble with vibration. The rest of the cup bowl is tackled next, rounding down as far as possible before it becomes necessary to remove some of the obstructing wood at the neck.

The action of the gouge in rounding is exactly opposite to its use when hollowing or coving, as I shall now explain.

Rounding over to the Left

It has been mentioned in the chapter on bowl turning that *pulling* a gouge along its path by the fingers can lead to trouble in digging in, so it is recommended that the gouge should always be pushed. In rounding over to the left the right hand should therefore be on the hand-rest, and the left hand holding the handle. Some of my pupils had two left hands, but so far I've managed to cope with anything.

It is quite possible for a right or left-handed turner to do good work without changing hand position, but it always looks wrong to me, and I hold the belief that after many years of doing a job, the job itself manages to teach the worker the best way of accomplishing it.

The starting position is with the bevel of the gouge resting on the highest point of the wood, the bevel rubbing the wood but the edge not yet cutting. The tool is at right angles to the lathe. The right hand is curled around the blade but is also on the rest, so the fingers are not able to encircle it completely. The closer the fingers are to the cutting edge the more control is gained. The right hand and rest are used as a pivot through which the gouge can be swivelled and the deepness of the cut is governed by the movement of the handle. The right hand does not move along the rest during the course of any one cut. When the lathe is started nothing will

81a. Shaping outside of egg cup. Bevel of pointed spindle gouge resting on wood at start of cut to the left.

81b. Shaping outside of egg cup. Gouge now cutting to left, handle lifting and swivelling up to the right to control quickness of curve, bevel rubbing at all times.

occur until the bevel is brought down and the handle lifted at the same time until the centre of the gouge starts to cut, with the bevel still rubbing the wood. Try a practice start-cut by rotating the lathe by hand and thereby seeing in slow motion exactly what is occurring. The handle continues to lift, the left hand twisting it clockwise, and at the same time bringing it up in an arch towards the right. This will result in a rounding cut to the left, the more the handle comes up and is twisted, the quicker the curve of cut. This triple action keeps the bevel rubbing the wood and following the cutting edge. After a few cuts, the waste wood to the left will offer too much resistance to further progress so it must be removed with the gouge by performing a *hollowing* action from the other direction. (Refer back to use of spindle gouge.)

82a. Roughing down to round, leaving a flange for fixing into the coil grip chuck so as to leave the tailstock end free.

82b. Cylinder firmly held by chuck so that hollowing out can be achieved.

82c. The head of the goblet is fashioned first, followed by the base, and the thin stem tackled last.

Design Completion

A ¼″ spindle gouge to complete the neck, a parting tool, beading and parting tool, and the ½″ gouge should be all that are needed to produce the finished goblet. The beading and parting tool is used for rounding over the small areas at the base. There are a myriad designs of goblets—one of my friends has a collection of 320 hardwoods, all turned into small cups, and all in different shapes. Try simple ones first.

Finishing and Parting Off

The completed work is sanded by 100 grit, followed by 150 grit, and in the case of very fine-grained wood, a perfectionist touch of 220. Sanding sealer follows, dried by friction and sanded off again with 320 grit. White friction polish gives a quick shining finish, but is not moisture proof, neither is wax.

Teak oil could be used where indicated (see page 68), Rustins Clear Plastic Finish, or a matt polyurethane.

Parting off is done in the same way as the handle for tools, making sure that the base of the goblet is cut flat or slightly concave so that it will stand firmly. If there is sufficient waste room, the point of the large skew chisel or Roy's parting tool can be used to clean up the end-grain of the base and part it off at the same time (see page 119).

Matching Sets

When comparing one object with another that is supposed to be similar in every detail, the eye is very quick to see discrepancies in height and diameter. A rule and calipers are the tools needed to ensure that each cup is made to the same measurements as far as these two dimensions are concerned. There is also the template method, and a combination of the two methods in which a scale drawing is made on squared graph paper. The drawing is then blocked-out using the squares just outside the outline of the cup to produce a series of squares, oblongs and rectangles that enclose the design and so provide reference points for caliper measurements.

These reference points are cut into the wood with the parting tool after the wood has been brought to a cylinder that is the same size as the largest diameter of the work. After this has been done, there remains only the job of joining up the reference points with curves. In this the eye is less discriminating, and the curves of each cup can be widely dissimilar without anyone noticing. (For more details about making matching copies, see chapter 20.)

15. Peppermills

Judging from the number of mechanisms I am asked to supply, the making of peppermills seems a popular pastime with amateur turners. It takes comparatively little wood so the rarer varieties such as rosewood are not too expensive to use, but good alternatives are ash, beech, utile, teak, walnut (very popular), and cherry. Three average sizes are known as 4″, 6″ and 8″ mills, although the actual mechanisms are slightly shorter than these sizes.

A method of making the bodies is by the use of a plain screw-chuck and hardwood plugs—the stages of turning must be followed in strict sequence. The 6″ mill is described and a 7″ length of stock 2½″ × 2½″ sawn is suitable for this. The 4″ needs a length of 5″, the 8″ a length of 9″.

The wood is put between centres and taken down to a cylinder with the ¾″ or 1½″ half-round roughing out gouge, a tool which is ground straight across instead of the normal 'nose' of a spindle gouge, so that all the edge can be used without any point to get in the way, and no fear whatsoever of digging in. The gouge has a short bevel of 45 degrees and will leave an exceedingly clean and smooth finish if it is pointed slightly up so that the bevel rubs the work and the gouge cuts instead of scraping. It is hardly necessary to clean up the surface with the chisel—this should make some readers smile with relief! The wood is slightly hollowed at the tailstock and 'squared off' at the driven end (parting tool will do this), then parted through 4″ from the tailstock to provide the body length, the remaining piece is sufficient for cap and waste (Fig. 84.1).

At D the body has to be centrally drilled ⅝″ deep with a 1″ diameter drill to take the notched mill-end. A handy bit for this is one of the flat quick boring ones obtainable either singly in different sizes, or in a set of bits with one interchangeable arbor. Another useful drill for lathe work is the

83. Peppermills.

normal carpenters' bit with the brace end sawn off so that it will go into the drill-chuck. The screw threads of the bit point must be blunted with a file so that there is no tendency for the bit to pull itself in when used in the lathe. The best bit to use for this sort of work is easily the Saw Tooth Machine Centre Bit described on page 22. The drill and chuck is used in place of the tail-centre, the body of the mill put between centres, the lathe run at lowest speed, and the hole can now be drilled to depth by screwing in the tailstock wheel.

The bit is then replaced with one ¾″ diameter and the hole drilled another ½″ or so deeper. By this method a flange is formed inside the body so that the notched mill-end is nicely seated at the proper depth from the end of the body (Fig. 84.2, D).

A hardwood plug slightly tapered is made to fit in the hole at D so that the body can be driven by the fork chuck. With this in position and a 1¼″ or 1⅛″ drill used in the tailstock as before, another hole is drilled down to meet the smaller holes. Another tapered plug is now needed for this end. These plugs can be kept and used again and again—there is no need to hammer them home each time they are used, as the slight taper will provide ample friction for drive purposes. It may be that with all this drilling, the body will go off strict centre, but this is immaterial at this stage. When both plugs are in position, the gouge is used to correct any 'off-centring', the ends trimmed square again if necessary, and a flange turned at C ¼″ wide and about ⅜″ deep. This forms a bearing for the cap (Fig. 84.4). It will be noted that at this stage the body is still just a plain cylinder in shape.

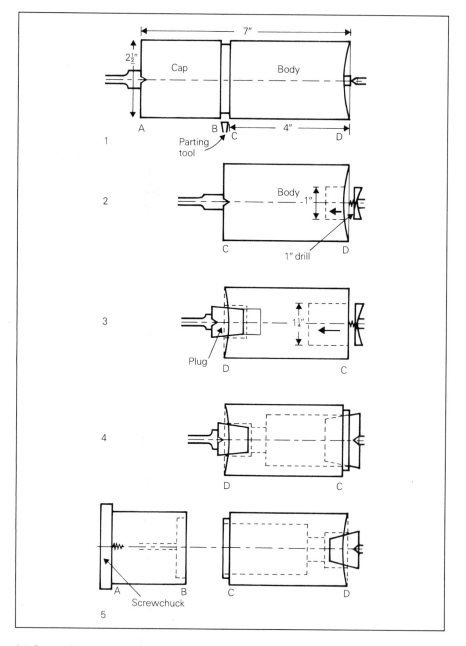

84. Stages in turning peppermills.
1. Between centres, body being parted off from cap.
2. Body between centres, drilling to accommodate mechanism mill-end.
3. Body plugged and reversed between centres, other end being drilled as container for peppercorns.
4. Body between centres, flanged at top end for cap fitting.
5. Cap in screw-chuck, partially drilled and recessed, and body being brought up to fit cap, the whole being supported by tail centre for finish-turning, shaping and polishing.

85. Bringing down from square to a cylinder 1½" half-round roughing out gouge, bevel rubbing and bringing off shavings.

86. Base already drilled and plugged and held by fork centre. Body being drilled at other end for peppercorn container. Note base hollowing, so that there will be no possibility of inserted mechanism standing 'proud' of base when fitted.

87. Flanging body to take cap. Top of parting tool, just appearing over revolving centre. Flange can be more determined by shadow at bottom of work.

88. Recessing cap to fit body. Body in foreground for testing fit at intervals. Recess is formed by pushing in parting tool. Scraping across the work may strip wood from screw-chuck.

89. Hollowed out body and cap fitted together for finish-turning. First line (emphasised for photo) shows join between body and cap. Second line shows final length of peppermill. About ¼" of threaded stem should protrude from finished mill.

90. Mill completely shaped by toolwork and being parted down to minimum holding dowel so that it can be completely sanded and polished while still held between centres.

The Cap

The piece for the cap is put on the screw-chuck A at the screw-end. It is slightly hollowed at face B and by using the parting tool gently, face B is recessed so that the flange of the body is a tight fit in it. The recess can be slightly deeper than the flange to ensure that cap and body meet well. Using a drill to help make the recess is not recommended, as it is end grain and the strain can quite easily strip the wood from the screw-chuck. Pushing the parting tool into the wood rather than scraping it across the face seems to work the best. When the recess is just too tight for the body flange, judicious use of garnet paper will ensure the close fit required. Then an $1/8''$ hole is drilled centrally through the recess, not far enough to foul the screw-chuck. This starts the hole, for completion later, when the stem of the mechanism is to be fitted. The cap is left on the screw-chuck and the body fitted to it, with the tailstock centre brought up as support. The whole mill can now be turned to the desired shape, remembering that the cap will need to be parted off at a length sufficient to allow about $1/4''$ of the threaded metal stem to protrude. The completed length of this mill is in fact $5\frac{1}{2}''$.

To facilitate sanding and polishing on the lathe, the end of the cap is taken down to a dowel about $1/2''$ diameter which will still leave sufficient drive to allow the final touches to the shape and the finish. This can be sander/sealer followed by a very small quantity of friction polish, plain wax finish, or teak oil burnished dry with a clean cloth.

The cap is then completely parted off the screw-chuck and the hole in it completed and enlarged to take the threaded stem easily. The metal washer with the square hole is pinned or screwed centrally into the cap recess. Small notches are chiselled into the base of the body to receive the metal retaining bar for the mill-end.

Mechanisms for peppermills can be supplied by the author, Peter Child, The Old Hyde, Great Yeldham, Halstead, Essex, England.

16. Automatic Tea Dispenser

The body of the one made here is out of 5″ × 5″ elm stock 9″ long, and holds an enormous quantity of tea. This suits our household because we are addicted to the beverage, but smaller models can be made and all can be designed to deliver the exact quantity of tea required straight into the pot. Again, this model is hand-held over the pot, but there is no reason why they should not be wall-mounted and the pot taken to the dispenser. The plunger is operated by a length of clock spring, the wooden button at the bottom of the plunger provides a stop to any further upward movement, and the waisted portion of the plunger collects the required quantity of tea to be delivered at each downward stroke. More tea?—more waist! The flange at A, Fig. 92.1, provides a stop to the downward stroke.

Plunger

This is made from 1¾″ square elm, 10″ long, mounted between centres and turned as Fig. 92.2. It is *not* parted off at this stage, because the centres are needed when the end AB has to be waisted. The hole for the clock spring can be made later, too.

Body

The 5″ × 5″ elm is mounted on a faceplate and turned to a cylinder almost the full length to the faceplate. The finished diameter will be about 4½″, Fig. 92.3. It is as well to bring up the tailstock as an additional support until the work is rounded down. A hole 2¼″ diameter is taken down ⅜″. This can be done with the parting tool cutting and scraping. Then a 1″ or 1¼″ hole is further carried down the whole length of the drill available, the drill being held in the tailstock, with the lathe at lowest speed and the drill fed in

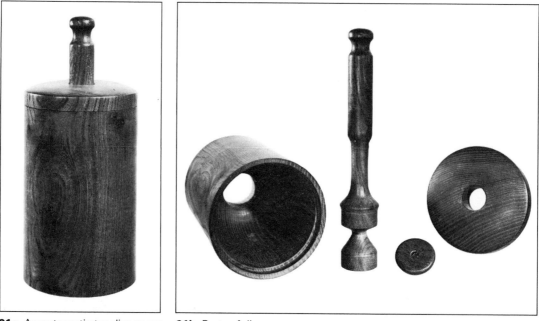

91a. An automatic tea dispenser.   **91b.** Parts of dispenser.

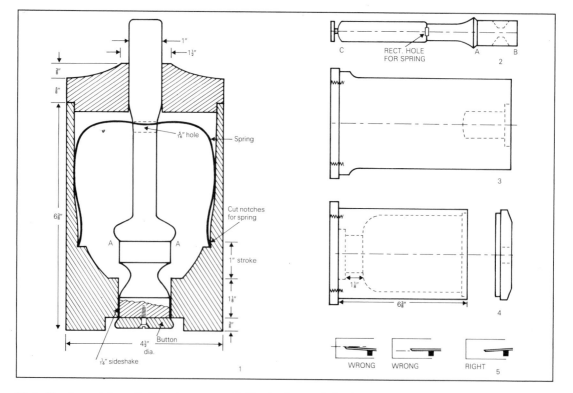

92. 1. The 'innards'.   2. The plunger.   3. The body.   4. Body reversed on faceplate, lid flanged and parted off, cavity drilled and scraped out.   5. Scraper to point slightly down when working.

93. Drilling base of container with carpenter's bit.

with the handwheel. This hole is then widened out with a suitable scraping tool until AB of the plunger can be fully inserted. The fit must not be too tight, $\frac{1}{32}''$ to $\frac{1}{16}''$ clearance is advisable all round. The body can then be taken off the faceplate and re-fixed the other way round, care being taken to fix it centrally. Fairly long screws, about 1″, should be used, as it is end grain and the scraping out of the body later exerts considerable force on them.

The lid is formed from the body length and before parting it off from the body, a hole is drilled through it in which can be fitted the end of the plunger, C, Fig. 92.4. Where possible in making articles with various components I try to fit the actual pieces into their respective holes rather than rely on measurement alone. A lazy way perhaps, but fairly sure! Again, a little bit of 'play' is advisable—I find this very easy to manage! After the lid is parted off, the body is cut to length and lipped to take the flange off the lid.

Now try to get a good fit for the lid, because then it can be jammed on to the body and the whole treated as a solid object which can be shaped and trimmed on the outside as desired, and sealed and polished much more easily, but don't blame me if there is difficulty in getting the lid off again. However, the cavity for the tea has to be made first, and a rounded scraper

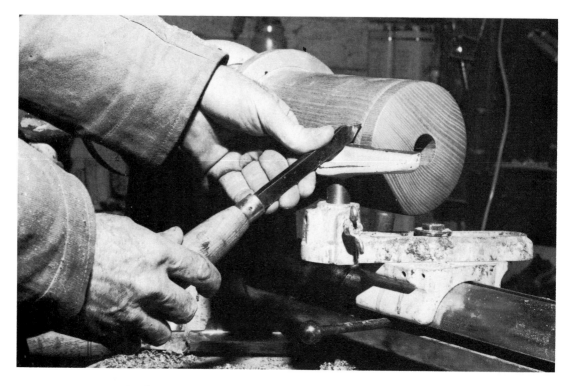

94. Cutting flange of container lid before parting off from body.

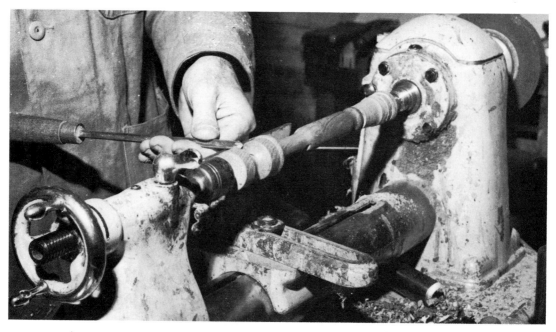

95. Removing wood from plunger to increase capacity. Note roughing-out gouge on lathe bed.

will get rid of most of the waste. There is an element of danger here because the hand-rest cannot be taken into the hole and has to remain placed across and as close as possible to the rim of the body. The farther the scraper goes down into the cavity the more of its length is over the hand-rest and it can dig in very quickly and without much warning, sometimes breaking the scraper tool if it is not a particularly robust one. My own scrapers have been made to my design and specifications by a good tool firm and they are forged from $\frac{3}{8}''$ thick special steel.

What also makes for better working is to position the height of the hand-rest so that the scraper tool is pointing slightly down to the centre of the work, Fig. 92.5.

The cavity is deepened until a length of $1\frac{1}{8}''$ of the second hole drilled from the other side is left for the plunger. This can be checked, using a flexible ribbon steel pocket rule by hooking the end over the bottom of the hole and reading off the length. The cavity is then sanded, the lid jammed on and the outside finished.

A piece of clock spring $\frac{5}{16}''$ wide $\times$ $10''$ long provides the spring plunger mechanism. A rectangular hole to take it is made as in Fig. 92.1, the clock spring slipped through it and bent as in the photograph. Two notches are chiselled into the sides of the cavity and the spring wedged in as Fig. 92.1. A small elm button $\frac{1}{4}''$ thick by $1\frac{5}{8}''$ diameter is turned with the grain running across the face and fixed as Fig. 92.1. With this in position the spring can be checked—there should be just over $1''$ of stroke.

The plunger is dismantled, put back in the lathe and AB shaped as shown by the dotted lines in Fig. 92.2, but as the amount of wood taken away determines the quantity of tea delivered, so only a little should be removed at first and the container then tested with tea in it to check the quantity let out. More wood can then be removed as required, and the plunger can be parted off finally from the lathe.

Finish

I am not in favour of having any chemical finish inside a food container and consider that a good sanded finish is quite satisfactory. My wife has a turned wooden box, slightly cracked (she gets all the rejects) in which she keeps kitchen salt. The lid is quite loose-fitting but despite all weather and steamy kitchen conditions, the salt remains for ever dry and loose. I put this down to the fact that the box was left natural and only sanded; and the wood keeps any moisture from the salt. The outside of the tea container was given a coat of sander/sealer, lightly sanded when dry, and then a dull carnauba/beeswax finish which is very durable and does not mark. When you have done all this—you can reward yourself with a cup of tea!

17. Cheese or Chopping Board

This project is a simple exercise in faceplate and between-centre turning, can be finished in a craft session, and is extremely useful in the home. Sycamore or beech are suitable, with a contrasting dark hardwood as a handle. For size, 1″ × 8″ × 8″ planed stock for the board, and 1″ × 1″ sawn turns down to a good handle size.

An 8″ diameter circle is drawn on the square board and the corners cut off. The nearer to a circle the square is made by doing this the better, as the chatter caused by the gouge taking off the edges on the lathe can be disconcerting and there is a slight possibility that the gouge be allowed to dig in one of them, taking out a chunk. The work is screwed directly to the faceplate if this is of less diameter than the board. On some lathes the faceplate is very much larger, in which case a disc of scrap wood is fixed between plate and board.

The board is turned to a disc, with a short-bevelled ⅜″ deep fluted bowl-turning gouge. An important difference is that this gouge is ground and sharpened straight across the edge and has not therefore got the point of a gouge used for between-centre work. It is used pointing well up, or handle well down, so that the short bevel is rubbing on the wood and cutting small curled shavings off.

To give a better finish only fine cuts should be taken. As no force is required, full concentration can be directed to seeing that the bevel of the gouge is rubbing on the wood, therefore the gouge takes over and more or less does it itself.

A straight scraper will do the job of bringing the work down to a disc, but it is not the right tool and can make an awful ragged mess of the grain on two sides of the round. By all means finish off the gouge work with a keen scraper but do not use it to take off quantities of wood.

96. Cheese or chopping board.

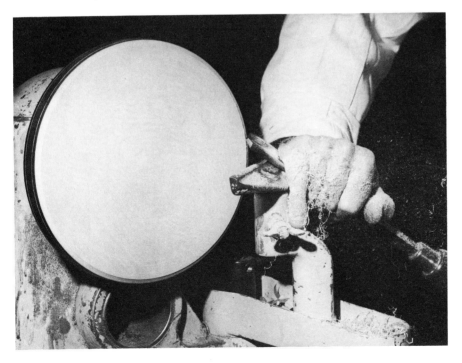

97. Turning off edge of disc to remove all traces of spread-over stain.

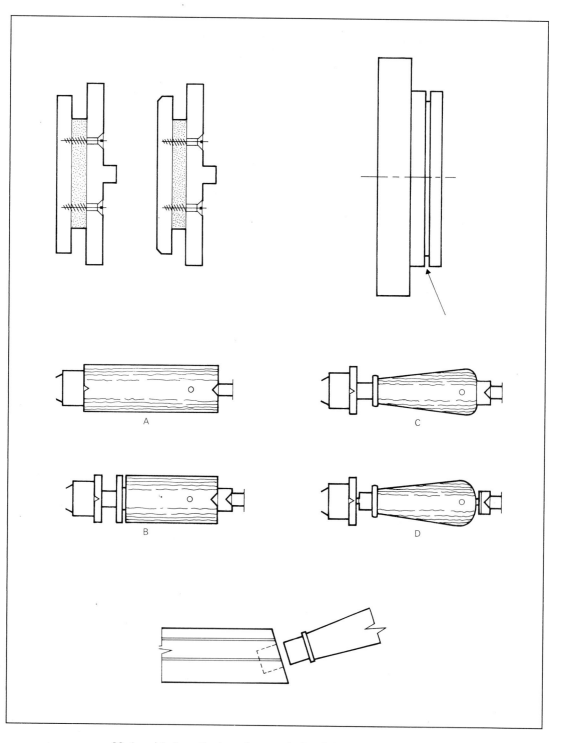

98. 1 and 2 show the faceplate work; 3 a-d show the stages in turning the handle; the method of fixing the handle can be seen at 4.

The side is then sanded on the lathe to a smooth finish and stained to the colour of the hardwood handle by applying a stain-dampened cloth to the revolving work and ignoring any stain that will inevitably creep on to the face. Medium pressure with the cloth will help to dry the stain and give a burnish to the side of the disc. Enthusiastic pressure will scorch the work, set fire to the cloth, and be painful to the user! Decoration can then be applied by scoring the side with the sharp point of a scraper or skew chisel exposing rings or beads of bare wood again.

A bevelled cut with the gouge or scraper from the side of the disc on to the face edge will remove all traces of stain that may have crept over, and leave a clean edge again. Since the stock has already been planed, no other treatment is required on the face beyond sanding it while it revolves. This can best be done by wrapping the garnet paper round a flat piece of wood or a cork block and holding it flat to the face so that it is sanded level.

The work is removed from the faceplate and a segment sawn off at a slight angle, say 10 degrees from the vertical. This is left straight from the saw at this stage, and the back of the disc stained and the screwholes filled.

Handle

This starts of as a piece of 1″ × 1″ sawn dark hardwood about 4″ long. A 3/16″ hole is drilled through the side about 1″ from one end. This is to hold a thong loop for hanging the board up in the kitchen and it is easier to drill the rectangular stock than wait until it has been turned. The piece is placed between centres and shaped as desired, or whichever way the tool should slip! A plain one is shown. The fixing dowel is ½″ diameter by ½″ long. When shaped it is sanded, given a rub of sealer which can be dried with a cloth pad while revolving, and finished with friction wax or perhaps a touch of friction polish. Each end of the handle is taken down gently with the parting tool to about ⅛″ diameter, removed from the lathe and the stalks pared off with a chisel.

A ½″ diameter hole is drilled into the centre of the segmented board. Brace and bit should be held upright to the face but a slight inaccuracy in angle does not matter. The handle is inserted and if it does not fit flush, the edge of the board is planed to suit, and then the handle can be glued into place.

18. Cheese Serving Board

Among the benefits of a progressive civilisation is our growing appreciation of good living. One of the indications of good living is a selection of cheeses at the end of a meal, and if your wife can serve these on a platter which has separate sections for each cheese—Gorgonzola, Camembert, Edam, Lancaster, and so on—then she will indeed be recognised as a grand hostess.

The serving board described in this chapter has six sections—though the heading picture shows one which I made with four—but the number can be chosen to suit requirements.

The board comprises a circular base, in this case elm, with a centre pillar. On the base rest six segments of a sycamore disc each with its own handle so that the section, with its particular cheese, can be lifted off the board. The centre pillar has a flange near the base under which the segments fit when in position.

Let us begin with the base board. This is made from a 10″ disc of elm, 1″ thick, planed and sanded flat one side, and to this side is screwed a 6″ faceplate. The edge of the disc is rounded, saucer-like, towards the faceplate with a ½″ or ⅜″ long and strong, deep fluted bowl-turning gouge and finished off with a heavy scraper tool.

The hole in the centre is 1″ diameter and ⅞″ deep and can be made by brace and bit, or by using a long and strong parting tool in a 'push and scrape' action. The face of the disc is then sloped evenly from rim to hole so that the centre is lower than the rim by ¼″. Most of this can be done with the gouge and finished with a straight-across heavy scraper.

The base is sanded, treated to a coat of sanding sealer, allowed to dry hard, then rubbed down with No. 000 grade wirewool, with possibly a trace

99. Cheese serving board.

of wax added. When removed from the faceplate, the screw holes in the bottom can be concealed under a 6″ diameter circle of self-adhesive baize.

The segments are made from an 11″ diameter disc of sycamore, 1″ thick, planed and sanded flat one side and screwed, like the base, to a 6″ faceplate. However, in this case, a disc of scrap wood is interposed between sycamore and faceplate so that a hole can be made right through the centre of the sycamore without damage to the metal faceplate.

The edge of the sycamore disc is trimmed straight with gouge and heavy scraper, then the front is 'faced' and sanded flat. If the lathe is provided with an indexing attachment it will be a simple matter to mark out on the face the lines dividing it into segments. A compass will do the job if the lathe is not so equipped.

The segments then have to be equally divided again and these lines continued down the edge to mark the locations for the holes of the handle dowels. These holes are placed in the centre of the edge, and are ³⁄₈″ diameter and ⁵⁄₈″ deep. The holes have to be drilled radially so that when

100. Boring the hole in the elm base board to receive the dowel of the centre pillar.

101. Using parting tool to widen hole in the sycamore disc from 1¾" to 2" at the top.

the handles are fitted, the whole set-up resembles a ship's wheel. Radial drilling can be accomplished by incorporating the hand-rest and a simple jig, or simply by eye with the aid of an assistant.

The edge of the disc is rounded slightly towards the faceplate, which improves appearance and also cleans up the holes.

A 1¾″ diameter hole is bored right through the centre of the sycamore disc, then widened out with a parting tool on the face to 2″ diameter, tapering to 1¾″ at the other side. This allows the segments to fit snugly around the central pillar when they are placed on the sloping surface of the base.

The sycamore is given a sealer finish, removed from the faceplate, screw holes are filled with white Brummer stopping, then it is sanded and sealed. After separation into the individual portions the edges are planed smooth and finished.

The centre pillar is made from a 7″ length of 2½″ square elm (or other hardwood such as iroko or afrormosia would be suitable), turned between centres to a cylinder with the roughing-out gouge and shaped in the stages shown. It is sander sealed, finished and parted off.

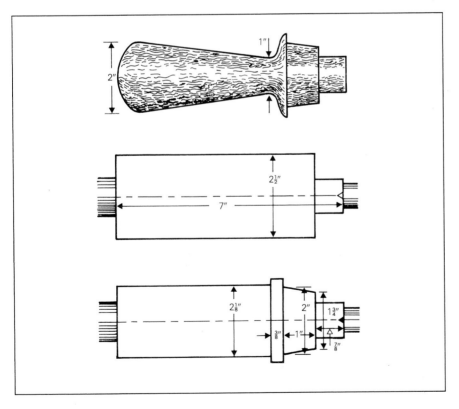

102. Shaping central pillar.

103. Trying pillar in tapered hole, then in blind hole of elm disc.

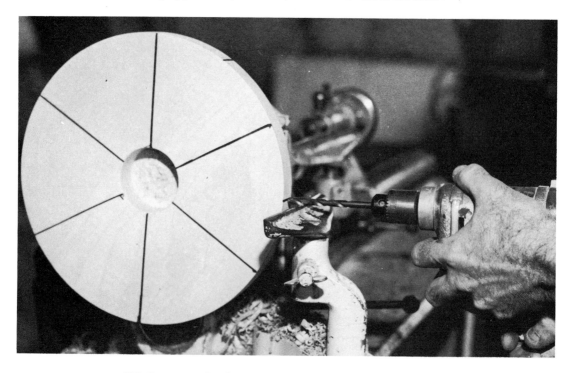

104. Sycamore disc fixed to faceplate while handle holes are bored.

Measurements can go awry, and easier and better results can be obtained if the handle is taken off the lathe at suitable intervals and tested for fit in the base: first for the bottom dowel, then for comfortable fit of the segments around the spindle.

Segment handles are turned from 4″ lengths of 1½″ square wood, similar to that used for the pillar. They are turned between centres to a simple sloping curve, terminating at the tailstock end in a ⅜″ dowel which should be a tight fit in the holes of the segments.

All that remains now is to glue the pillar to the base, and the segment handles in their holes.

19. Table and Standard Lamp Bases

Like the egg cup, designs of these bases must run into hundreds, and all of them can be attractive, but the chosen shape must include two essential requirements, stability and proportion. A tall, slender table lamp base may look good but if it falls over at a slight touch then it has indeed fallen down on the requirements of stability. Small, squat designs can also be well shaped but it may be very difficult to find a shade that will do an adequate shading job without also concealing most of the base.

Lamps with a slender or long column need a wide base so they are made in two parts, the bottom turned on a faceplate and a central hole drilled through; the column is turned between centres with a turned dowel to fit into the hole in the base. Lamp bases can be turned from one piece of wood provided it is thick enough, and in my opinion the wood should be at least $4'' \times 4''$ or larger. Turning should begin by setting up the wood between centres and rounding down to a cylinder with the roughing-out gouge. The hole for the flex should be drilled next, before any shaping is done, and this is a simple job with a lamp standard shell auger of $5/16''$ diameter bit. It is used with a guide and support set up in the lathe. The end of the auger is of a special shape without any point, and this, provided that it is not hindered, will bore its way through the exact centre of revolving wood without wandering. It is difficult for the amateur to sharpen the cutting edges of the auger without giving them some vestige of a 'lead' and this can then make the auger drill out of true, so sharpening is not recommended. My own is ten years old, has never been sharpened, but still performs accurately albeit a trifle reluctantly. The hole of the boring guide is deliberately made oversize, so that the auger is self-compensating for any slight inaccuracy in lining up the equipment or in the lathe itself.

One way of using the auger is to take careful measurements and drill the wood to within ½″ of the driving centre. Care is needed here, or both driving centre point and auger will suffer by collision. The remaining ½″ of hole is drilled by hand methods. The other way, preferable in long stock, is to drill halfway from both ends. When one half has been drilled, the stock is taken from the lathe, reversed and set up again. A snag is that there is now a nice round hole instead of the solid wood needed to accommodate the point of the driving centre. This hole can be plugged temporarily with a short piece of dowel, or a special driving centre known as a counterbore used in place of the 2 or 4 jaw driving centre. This tool is equipped with a ⁵⁄₁₆″ metal spindle that goes into the hole in the wood, and the counterbore is given a smart tap to make its prongs enter the wood and form a drive.

The counterbore tool is basically a drill and in this capacity extremely useful when making lamp bases. It is used instead of the normal 2 or 4 jaw driving centre and the drilled wood is set up between lathe centres with the spindle just inserted into the base of the lamp. The tail centre is a plain or revolving cone. With the wood held firmly by one hand, the lathe is started at its lowest speed and the wood brought up to the full length of the spindle by slowly screwing up the tail wheel. Since the wood cannot revolve, the counterbore, instead of driving, will start drilling and the idea is to allow drilling to continue until all the drilling head of the counterbore is buried in the wood so that only the shank is showing outside. Then the restraining hand releases the wood sharply, the counterbore ceases to drill and commences to drive, so that shaping of the lamp can be started. It will be seen that there is a small clearance between the shank of the driving counterbore and the surrounding wood, so that a long and strong parting tool can be used to cut the base straight, or better still, slightly curving inwards. Thanks to the small clearance, all the waste wood can be removed completely without damage to tool or shank of counterbore, and the lamp base will need no other treatment to ensure that it stands firmly. This action cannot be undertaken if the ordinary driving centre is used, since this is in the way of the parting tool and therefore the base has to be cleaned up by hand after it has been taken from the lathe.

Another use for this useful tool is when joining two or more pieces of wood together, e.g. in the making of a long standard lamp. The pieces are pre-drilled for the flex as already described, and one piece held so that the counterbore drills in at least 1″ to form a round mortice. The piece is then released, the wood revolves, and work can be done to shape it. The other piece, centred on its holes in the lathe, is cut down at one end to form a dowel which will fit into the mortice; the flex hole runs unimpeded right through; the pieces, when assembled, will line up, and a couple of small beads worked at the joint will conceal any slight discrepancy in the meeting place.

Nipples for Lamp-Holders

Two types are available, usually made from brass. One has a short threaded spigot which takes the lamp-holder, and a flat round plate with three screwholes by which the nipple is secured to the wooden top. The objection is that the screws cannot find much hold in end grain, and unless the plate is recessed into the wood, the finished appearance can be clumsy. The type of nipple I prefer is really a very short tube of brass, half of it threaded to take the lamp-holder, the other with a much coarser thread suitable for holding in wood. Using pliers or grips to screw this into the wood can do irreparable harm to the other threads. The square tang of a file can be used as a screwdriver, or the nipple, which is $\frac{3}{8}''$ diameter can simply be hammered into the $\frac{5}{16}''$ hole in the wood. In hardwood, this gives a satisfactory hold, but a touch of epoxy resin glue will make good if for any reason the hold is weak.

Lamp Base Stock Material

If time allows, unseasoned wood can be utilised for bases. It is cheaper and can possibly be obtained from the sawmill cut to $5'' \times 5''$ thickness, and in $18''$ lengths. This thickness, when turned down, makes very stable bases, but would be difficult to obtain in seasoned stock since normal sizes go from $4'' \times 4''$ to $6'' \times 6''$. The latter size is a little too big for most lathes to swing comfortably. Each $18''$ length is rounded to a cylinder and drilled for flex, using the counterbore drill method, then laid aside to dry out, the hole down the middle speeding up this process considerably. When dry, the stock can be cut into material for $6''$ lamps, $9''$ lamps, $12''$ lamps, or any like combination. Some amount of splitting at the ends of the cylinders may occur when drying out, but if the timber is regularly inspected, any cracks that have started can be discouraged from spreading by deeply notching the end of the crack at right angles with a chisel. Waxing or painting the ends with thick paint may also help.

Standard Lamp Bases

These need to be fairly large in diameter, and sometimes quite thick for design purposes. Small boards can be edge-joined to provide the width but this method ruins the run of the grain. Wider thin boards are more easily obtainable than thick ones, and a good base can be built up by employing one or more thicknesses as in the following example.

Two discs, say $9''$ and $12''$ diameter, are used, the smaller one fitting into

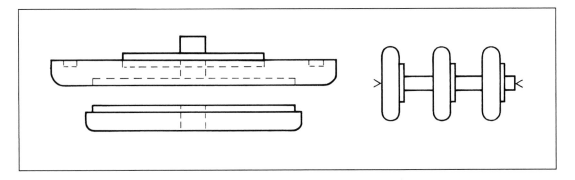

105. Base and feet of standard lamp.

the top of the other by recessing. It can be 1″ thick and is turned and finished as per the diagram. It is best to polish each disc separately, and white polish or one of the clear plastic finishes would be suitable.

The main base, also 1″ thick, is first recessed to receive a faceplate and can be marked for positions of small feet, three at 120 degree centres, ⅞″ from outside edge. On the Myford this is easily done by using the radiusing device incorporated in the end pulley and stop plunger. Then the disc is reversed and the faceplate screwed into the recess made for it. The face is now recessed ¼″ deep, in the centre so that the smaller disc will just fit, with the flanged rebate sitting down nicely all round. The two discs, with the grain lined up, are glued together, the flange left without glue. Any future slight movement between the discs will not then show, as no unpolished line will be revealed. Future movement (warping) will be restricted if the discs are fitted, one heart side up and the other heart side down. The completed base is centrally drilled with 1″ bit to take the dowel of the stem, removing the polish round the hole so that the glue will take when fitted.

Base Legs or Feet
Three circular ones can be turned out of one piece held between centres and polished on the lathe before parting off. Their short dowels are glued and screwed into holes drilled for them in the base. When the lamp is assembled, the flex at the base should be clamped to the side of the flex hole with a short piece of dowel.

Bottle Lamp
This wood was dry, 3″ thick by 6″ wide by 8″ long. A bandsaw was used to cut it into the rough shape of a flask, a centre hole bored, and then it was mounted lengthwise between centres, to shape the two 3″ sides first. An

electric filament lamp has to be used behind the lathe and facing the turner. This shows up the two revolving sides as shadows, and is essential for accurate tool placing in turning. Neon illumination is no good. Then the wood was faceplate mounted on one face by screws 1½″ away from the faceplate centre. This allowed the other face to be recessed and beaded to take a 3½″ diameter ceramic tile insert. The rest of the face was given a gentle curve. When finished, this face was now faceplate mounted, so that the other one could be similarly turned. The final operation, hiding the screw holes, was to fix in the two tiles. For this we used a tube of flexible white rubberised bath cement. If the recesses for the tiles are an accurate fit, there is danger later on of the wood moving slightly and cracking the ceramics, so the recesses are turned very slightly larger than the diameter of the tile. A thin coat of cement round the sides of the tile holds it firmly in place, and when dry is indistinguishable from the white tile surround.

106. The first stages in shaping the sides of the lamp from the rough band-sawn flask. Note the shadows of the revolving wood. These are more clearly seen if a filament lamp is placed behind the lathe bed. The finished lamp can be seen in the photograph on page 238.

20. Making Copies in Lathework

When only one or two copies have to be made, then a rule, pencil, and calipers should be the only measuring and marking tools needed, together with the article to be copied. If this is small and portable enough, say a drawer knob by itself, then it is useful to have it handily on the lathe bench for measurement and reference against the copy. However, it could be that a missing or damaged leg of a chair has to be replaced and in this case measurements have to be taken off and transferred to the work on the lathe. It does not always appear to turners that it is quite feasible to remove semi-finished work from the lathe and take it to the original for comparison, putting it back between centres for further work.

I have read somewhere that one side of the driving chuck should be given a distinct scratch or file mark so that work can be replaced exactly in the position it came off. In faceplate work this marking is definitely a good idea as the screwholes in the metal plate may not be exactly interchangeable, and each screw prefers its original bed, but between centres, with a driving centre in good order, and preferably a revolving centre in the tailstock, there must be some misalignment in the lathe itself if the work cannot be replaced in any choice of position without going out of true rotation.

The first task in copying is to find wood of big enough section and as long as the original, plus a margin for waste at the driving end. It is set up between centres, or the screw-chuck can be used in the case of a small knob, and turned down to cylinder with one of the roughing-out gouges.

The section of the original that has the largest diameter is measured off with calipers and all the duplicate length is turned down to this. The calipers should be of the spring screw type and be given a small extra

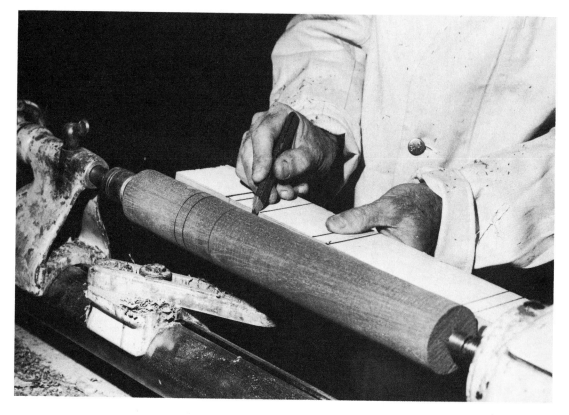

107a. *Copywork.*
Using a template to mark off salient points of the wine table leg, starting at tailstock end and leaving sufficient waste at headstock for parting off.

clearance to allow for finishing and sanding. Length measurements of the major quirks, beads and ends of curves on the original are then transferred, starting at the tailstock end, by means of a pencil held to the revolving wood and supported by the rest. A common error is to take off too many measurements in one go, and the resulting number of pencil lines around the duplicate can give rise to great confusion!

It is a sound basic rule of turnery that one always works from large to small diameters and not the reverse. This sequence is also best in copying.

Another error of a beginner is that he will try to copy a curve exactly without defining first the exact length and cutting down to exact depths at both ends *before* shaping the piece in between. If this is done carefully with the aid of calipers, rule, pencil and parting tool, then the curves worked in between would have to be woefully inaccurate to be easily seen in comparison with the original. A long, gentle curve can be divided into smaller lengths, using calipers and parting tool to cut down to the various

107b. *Copywork.*
Sighting a finished leg against a revolving copy in the lathe to check correctness of central bulb curve. Note that the beads and quirks at either end of the curved bulb have been completed first to ensure that the length of the bulb is correct before final attention is paid to the actual curve.

diameters. The curve can then be done in sections and then the whole trimmed down. The best tool to fashion these long curves is the large roughing-out gouge, used on one of its sides. If the original is portable it can be held in front of the revolving duplicate and the curve 'sighted' and adjusted accordingly. This is of great help.

Templates

These are of use when many copies are required. A simple type is just a length of narrow hardboard or plywood marked with lines corresponding to the key points of the original shape. This is held on the rest, edge against the revolving wood and the points transferred with a pencil. A refinement is to insert fine panel pins part way into the side of the plywood, nip off and sharpen the ends into points with a file. When held against the revolving wood these points will score it at the correct intervals.

108. Reproductions of mahogany wine tables.
The tripod spindle of the table on the left has been copied with the aid of a template.
Only the outline shape of the barley twist of the table on the right can be made with
the lathe. The cutting of the spirals has to be hand done.
Making the recessed table tops has been described elsewhere. To be an 'authentic
copy' the circumference of these tops must be the same as the circle containing the
feet of the three legs.

In my work for reproduction furniture makers, I had a constant demand
for pedestal legs all of one particular design. For these I made a full size
drawing on squared paper of half one side of a leg, pasted it on to plywood
and cut out the actual shape. This gave me the key points for transferring
to the wood and also by sighting across the template on to the wood I could
shape the curves exactly. Some recommend a template of this kind to be a
'reverse' one, presumably with the intention that it can be 'fitted' into the
duplicate. It does not seem to work for me.

Finally I must stress the need of sticking to accurate caliper measurements of the various thicknesses. There may be some optical illusion about
revolving wood that explains the odd fact that beginners soon get to the
stage of producing a reasonable facsimile but it is very often too small!

21. Jar Lids

Glass jars containing coffee, pickles, mustard, honey and various sauces, preferably with metal screw tops, can be quite decorative, and their appearance much improved, with or without contents, by enclosing the screw top in a wooden overcoat. A nice simple job, and a pleasing small present that could be offered in compensation for spending too much time in the workshop.

A disc of wood, thicker than the metal top, and slightly larger in circumference, is sawn out and fixed to the lathe on the screw-chuck. Being side grain, the screw has quite a good grip. An end grain piece *could* be used I suppose, but it will not be any the more beautiful in appearance and I never invite trouble.

The first task is to bring the disc down to complete round and the tool to use is the ⅜″ long and strong bowl turning gouge in the same way as truing up a disc for a bowl. The front to the disc is faced flat with the same tool, entering it on its side and cutting in a shallow arc to the centre. The straight scraper or scraping bar will finish off the edge, which can be slightly rounded, and also the face, which is better flat or a little concave. The face can also be decorated with one or two lines or fine beads done with an old, small, flat file ground to a sharply conical point. This provides one of the most useful shapes for delicate work. Using the point 'straight in' leaves a sharply defined V groove, and the curved side can be utilised to take off fine scrapings by drawing it across the surface of the work. This action is grand for cleaning end grain of the base of a small item, say a round box, the other end of which is only held by a wooden spigot or mandrel. A heavier, straight scraper would tend to exercise too much force, dig in, and wrench the work off centre. It will be apparent that the curved

109. A selection of lidded boxes and a wooden screw-topped jar lid. From left to right—kitchen salt container in elm, tobacco jar in mahogany, screw-top in elm, spices box in American hardrock maple.

side of a small scraper can only bring off tiny shavings as only a little of the edge can be cutting at any one time, and this is a great help in avoiding a dig-in.

Sanding follows, then sanding sealer, sanding, and any of the finishes already described, and then the work is taken off the screw-chuck, which is replaced by a faceplate on which has been mounted a scrap disc of wood about 1″ thick. This has to be recessed to take and hold the half-finished lid so that it too can be recessed to take the metal cap. Some sort of measuring tool could be used, inside calipers or what have you, but my practice is to set the rest across the face of the scrapwood disc and push in a beading and parting tool about 1/16″ and somewhere about what I think is the diameter required. I then stop the lathe and apply the wood lid to the scrap disc. This gives me a better idea of what I'm doing, so I start up and push the tool in again. Roughly three goes and I have what I want, the start of a recess just slightly too small for the wooden lid. Commencing from the centre left hand side (depending on rotation) of the disc, the tool is pushed in with a series of jabs, gradually coming out to the guide recess mark I have chosen out of the three. If any go beyond this I face up again with the scraper and remove all traces of them. The beading and parting tool can then be used in a 'jab and scrape' action, gradually deepening the recess

110. Facing across the round jar lid with a ⅜″ gouge, entered on its side and swept across to the centre with bevel rubbing in an arcing cut.

111. Decorating the top of the lid, using a 'steeple-point' scraper.

112a. The lid has been jammed into a recessed hole in a scrap wood disc. It is now being recessed to take the metal screwcap. The beading and parting tool is being used in a 'push and scrape' action from centre height to left side.

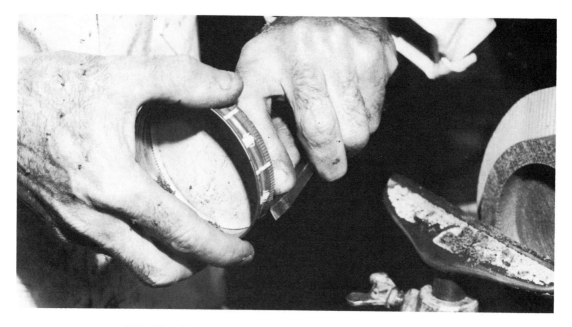

112b. Checking depth of recess against side of metal lid—a 'rough and ready' method but surprisingly accurate.

until it is about ½″ deep and flat. I nearly forgot, it is a good thing too to have a hole, say about 1″ diameter, right through the centre of the scrap disc—this comes in handy later on. Now the recess has to be very gradually widened out so that the wooden lid is a push fit into it. This takes care and patience as it is very easy indeed to make the recess oversized, remember that a ⅛″ cut widens the diameter by ¼″, double. If, despite reasonable care, the recess is too big, a strip of newspaper round the cover might fix the trouble, but usually it is best to face off and start again. Another method is to start of with a recess only ¼″ deep, and if too big, carry on recessing slightly smaller for another ¼″. Sloping the sides inward is not much use, as then they don't hold well, and can ruin the polished outside of the wooden cover.

When everything has gone well, the wooden cover can then be fitted into the recess, helped perhaps with a tap from a piece of wood, but make sure it 'bottoms', otherwise the finished job will be slightly drunken in shape. The cover itself has to be recessed to take the metal cap, and you will have had some practice by now. The idea is to sink it in flush with the turned up metal rim of the cap overlapping the wood as a tiny flange. Too loose and you will have to use glue which is a messy job, too tight and it might jam halfway down the recess. Before you swear at me, screw on the bottle and use it to ease out the jammed cover. A nice tight fit, then a week in the

112c. Checking fit of metal lid into recess. The rolled metal edge should not be allowed to enter the recess, but remain on the outside of the wood as a tiny flange.

warm kitchen, which will cause the wood to shrink slightly, and you will never get it out again, and of course you don't want to.

The final job is to remove the finished wooden lid from its snug fit into the scrapwood disc. Take the disc off the faceplate, insert a wad of newspaper into the central hole to protect the finish, then prod out the cover with a wooden piece of dowel or small tool handle.

Lids to Pottery Jars

Jars made of pottery never seem to be truly circular, slightly warped no doubt by the heat of the kiln. However, a fitting wooden lid can be made for them by using the following method. The screw-chuck can be used as before, the wood blank for the jar being turned down on the edge so that it finishes approximately the same diameter as the outside of the jar, maybe a little larger to disguise as far as possible the discrepancy between the true round of the lid and the slight ovalness of the jar rim. Then a scrapwood recess is made for the lid as described.

In a cheap job, or where thicker wood is unobtainable, the bottom of the lid is faced flat and the hole left by the screw can be filled flush with wood stopping. Where thicker wood is used, it can be thinned down with the gouge thereby removing all traces of the screw hole, before being faced flat. The thickness of the lid is then reduced further by making a flange of ⅜″ or ½″ thickness, cutting down with the parting tool to do this, and leaving a plug portion of the lid that is an *easy* fit into the pottery jar top. A notch has then to be cut into the edge of the plug to take a rubber sealing ring *edgeways* into it, so that some of the rubber protrudes all round. The normal sized parting tool is far too wide to be any good for this job, so I have ground the sides of one down, keeping to the original shape, until I have one only ⅟₁₆″ wide instead ot the more normal ¼″ standard tool. This is a tool well worth the trouble of making, since it comes in handy for all sorts of small jobs such as drawer pulls and miniature turnings.

If a rubber sealing ring of a suitable size is difficult to find, a substitute can be cut from a rubber sheet or old inner tube. With this in place in its notch in the plug, the wood lid can be made to fit reasonably tightly into the pottery jar.

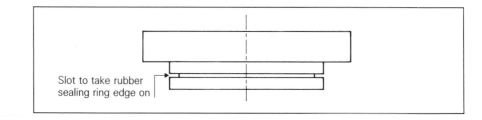

Slot to take rubber
sealing ring edge on

22. Shallow Dishes and Fittings

Various plates can be made fairly easily by following basic bowl-turning techniques. A big advantage is that 1½″ thick stock is ample and as such is easier to obtain in a seasoned state than thicker wood. If it is not fully dry it will without doubt twist out of shape after turning and this can be most disappointing. Time is a valuable servant of the turner and stock of this size should be cut into discs and left in the workshop for as long as possible before using. The alternative is to obtain seasoned 1½″ × 1½″ stock and glue sufficient lengths together to form a laminated or segmented board from which the disc can be cut. Different species can be alternated to give a striped or otherwise contrasting effect, and twisting in a composite board of this nature is minimal.

114. Table platter in afrormosia with circular pottery tile.

The quickest way to start the turning is to plane and sand one side flat and fix a faceplate centrally, with screws that only penetrate the wood by ¼″ to ⅜″ maximum. Another method is to fix a faceplate to one side by screws so placed that their holes will be removed when recessing for the fitting on the other side. In this method the central area of the base is flattened with gouge and scraper work and a shallow recess formed that will fit a faceplate. This method is also used when no screwholes are wanted anywhere in the finished work, and the partly turned disc is fixed to a faceplate by the glue and brown paper sandwich method described on page 81.

The edge of the disc is turned true with the long and strong gouge and rounded towards the base. This area should then be finished-scraped and sanded before any wood is removed from the face, because the thicker the wood worked on, the less trouble with vibration. Remembering a basic principle like this makes the work so much easier.

The next job is the recess for the fitting. The photographs show the turning of the round tile dish, but they all follow the same pattern in the beginning. The parting tool is used scraper-fashion to start a recess just too small for the tile. The waste wood is then taken out with the long and strong gouge and the bottom area flattened with the heavy straight scraper,

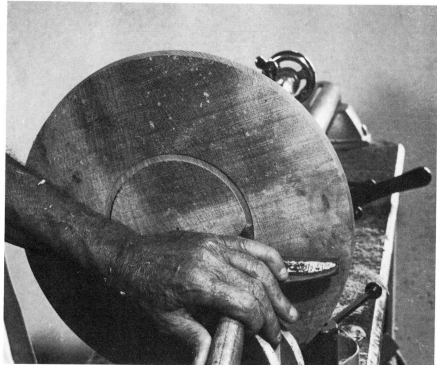

115a. First stage in turning the inner recess. The disc has been trued and rounded towards the faceplate in a saucer design. A parting tool is being used to mark out and deepen a recess just too small in diameter for the fitting to be used in it.

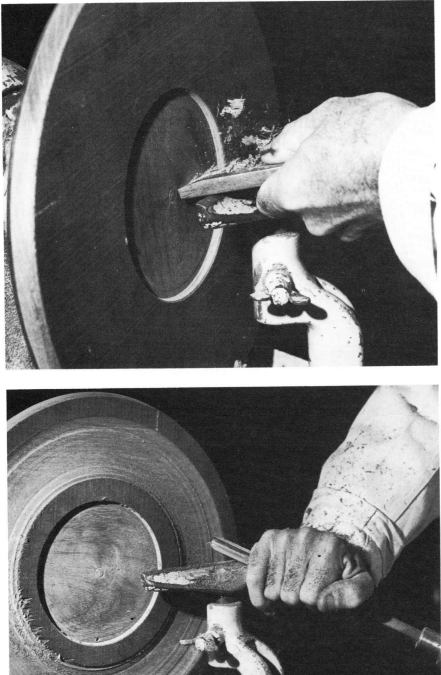

115b. Second stage. The heavy straight scraper used to deepen the recess to size. Note its downward angle. After this, the diameter of the recess is gradually widened—the fitting is frequently tested in it until it is the correct size.

115c. Third stage. Taking out waste wood to form the outer recess. Gouge must be entered on its side and taken towards the centre in a slight arc cut. *Right* hand pushing the gouge, left foot will be forward so that handle is resting on leg.

116. Shallow nut-cracker bowl. Inside recess for cracked shell, outer recess for unbroken nuts. In iroko, with brass ship's wheel cracking mechanism.

remembering to position the rest to allow the cutting edge to point *down* to the work.

My lathe is rotating clockwise and the edge of the scraper is placed exactly at centre height and presented to the *left* of the centre pip before traversing to the right. It will not cut at first, since the wood is travelling up from under, but this preliminary placing helps to ensure that the recess is finished flat. When it is deep enough, the diameter is very gradually widened with the scraper or parting tool until the tile is a good fit.

The tile should be later glued into its recess, and if the wood used is not well dry, there is a good chance of the tile cracking at a later date. From a design point of view, the surface of the tile should be slightly proud of the wood to allow easy cleaning. Similarly with the round butter dish. A tight fit for the latter is not good design, since the housewife may find difficulty in getting it out and back again.

When the inside recess is completed, and where the nutcracker unit is concerned, this means leaving a central mound for the bottom plate of the mechanism, the hollowing of the platter recess can begin, by using the long and strong gouge, entering it on its side, and cutting towards the inner recess. It will be discovered that the gouge cannot go all the way, because

117. Smoked glass butter and cheese platter in sycamore.

with each cut the wall of the inner recess begins to build up and jam the progress of the gouge. Trying to turn 'uphill' is to invite trouble, so soon the worker will have to reverse direction of cut and start hollowing from recess to outer edge.

Combining the two approaches will finally result in the required depth of platter recess and thickness of inner wall. In the cheese and nutcracker dishes, this is a hollow, to be finished with a rounded heavy scraper—in the tiled dish it is a flat and so a straight heavy scraper is the tool to use.

Finish-scraping the inside and outside of the recess walls can be a tricky operation, due to the smallness of the diameter and the way of the grain, which will be found to invite a dig-in, unless great care is used, a gentle approach, the rest at the proper height and close to the work. Sometimes the only way to clean up these walls without digging in is to use a sharp skew chisel with its widest side flat on the rest and only the long point used scraper-wise to remove very thin cuts.

It will be obvious that these turnings are a combination 'two-in-one' design. The nutcracker unit, butter dish, and tile would look quite well set in the small recesses alone—the platter extensions are an attractive variation.

23. Round Containers

There are two main problems here, the excavation of the interior, and the making of a well-fitting wooden cap or lid. The box described is a small one, since in a way these are more difficult to make than the larger variety, such as tea caddies or biscuit and tobacco jars.

The work is held in the clamp ring of the Myford chuck. If a chuck of this type is not available, an alternative is to use a small faceplate and screws, but remember that it is end-grain so two or three screws are needed and they should enter the timber by at least ½″. A screw-chuck alone is useless for this work, as drilling or scraping out the interior of the container exerts heavy strain on the fixings. Sufficient waste wood must be left at the base of the container so that parting off can be done without fouling the holding screws. Alternatively, the base of the container could be finished by hand before mounting on the faceplate with a thin scrap disc of wood between, to allow any slight rounding of the outside of the base of the container without damaging the metal faceplate. The screwholes in the finished job will have to be filled with stopper, or the whole base concealed with a baize cloth bottom.

The wood is turned down to a cylinder of the exterior size required, and the end faced up with the parting tool.

Lids

There are a number of ways of making these. One is to use an entirely different piece of wood, put it on a screw-chuck and first make the bottom of the lid complete with flange 'plug', sized to fit into the interior of the container when this has been turned. The hole left in the outer side of the lid by the screw can be drilled later and a separately made knob with a dowel glued into it.

118. The lid of a small container has been made 'back to front' and is now being parted off the main body.

Making a container by this method involves three separate operations—main container, lid and knob.

In large containers, the appearance of the whole is vastly improved if the grain of the wood runs right through from container to lid. To do this, the piece for the lid should be parted off from the main body first, working the flange plug and parting off at the base of this. The home-made, very narrow parting tool should be used, since it does not need much waste room, and the little bit of grain figure that is lost will not be noticed. The rough surface of the base of the plug will have to be cleaned up by hand off the lathe, or the scrapwood disc recess method used instead.

Yet another method of working the lid, useful in small containers where the run of the grain may not matter, is to work the flange plug first on the end of the main cylinder and then part off the thickness of lid required. The lid will then be fitted 'upside down'.

Notice that, in whatever method being used, all the lids are still unfinished at this stage, since there has been no way to get at the very top surface of the lid to finish it. Enlightenment will follow.

Now we are left with the main body of the container still on the lathe, with the unfinished lid portion loose and available for fitting into the interior when this has been hollowed out. It is advisable for the rebate of the lid flange to be made fairly deep, i.e. the container will have thick walls at first.

Hollowing the Interior

A lot of waste wood can be taken out by a suitable drill inserted in the tailstock. It is marked for depth and run at lowest speed since end-grain boring is very heavy work. In large containers the bowl turning gouge can be used to take out more waste.

The gouge must be used on its side (flute facing in), and it might be wise to make a starting groove with the point of a scraper at a diameter slightly less than that of the plug of the lid. The gouge, put into this to start its cut, will not be so liable to slip sideways and back before it has had the chance to enter the wood firmly and get a grip on it. The end grain is tough, and the gouge requires firm pressure to keep it cutting into the middle.

Then more waste can be removed by a round-nosed scraper. The rest should be put across the face of the hole, and at a height so that the scraper tool is pointing slightly down and the edge in contact with the wood at centre height. As excavation progresses, the rest may have to be additionally heightened to maintain this principle, and it is very important, so I will repeat, that a scraper should always 'trail', i.e. the handle is held higher than the work point. The degree of trail can make the difference between easy working and excessive roughness and vibration, so experiment with slight differences in height of rest, but there must always be *some* degree of trail, however slight.

For a container with a straight sided interior, the final finishing tool to use is a thick skew scraper. Only the long point and a very little of the cutting edge does any work. The scraper is put flat on the rest, 'lined-up' parallel to the side of the container, and pushed steadily into the interior, removing a maximum of ⅛″ cut at any one go (so the point and an ⅛″ of the edge is working only). The deeper the interior the more levering force is encountered as the length of the scraper protruding over the rest increases, so more downward force is needed at the handle end to keep the scraping point in position without being jerked downwards out of control.

In a small container, the *thickness* of the scraper may be too much for the radius of the interior, and so prevent the point from cutting, so this thickness should be relieved by a *very slight* ground off bevel on the side of the scraper.

When the interior diameter of the container is *just* too small to admit the plug of the lid, the scraping out of the interior is stopped. The bottom is then flattened and cleaned up by using a straight-across scraper, again employed in a trailing position. With a small box of any depth it is very difficult to see the cutting edge of the tool working and the correct action has more or less to be defined by 'feel' of the tool in the hands. This is one reason why small, deep boxes are more difficult to make than larger ones.

119a. The container is being drilled with a saw tooth machine centre bit, held still whilst being fed into the revolving work. Note depth mark on shank.

119b. The drilled hole is being widened, using a skew end scraping tool fed into the revolving work parallel with the side of the container, and in a trailing position, i.e. rest positioned so that the handle end of the tool is higher than the working point. The half-finished lid is on the lathe bed available for constant checking of size of container hole.

120. The lid is a jam fit into the container, and the friction of wood against wood allows work to be done on shaping the knob with a ¼" spindle gouge. The join between lid and container was invisible, but has been outlined for the photograph.

The interior of the container is now very firmly sanded with the object of removing sufficient wood so that the plug of the lid can be firmly fitted into it. This is a tricky business, requiring frequent stopping of the lathe and testing with the lid. It is so very easy to remove too much wood, thereby making the lid a poor fit. Success is when the lid can be firmly bedded into position by gentle blows with the side of the hand only. The object of all this is to convert the container back to a 'solid' cylinder, the friction of wood against wood gives ample hold for the work to be done on finishing the outside of the lid, in fact if this is left thick enough at the start, it is quite possible to fashion the end into a small knob, using a ¼" spindle gouge and small scraper.

The outside of the container and lid can now be cleaned up with a straight scraper, and the join between lid and container made almost invisible. Also, if the interior diameter has been determined first, more wood can be removed from the whole of the outside of the container, thus leaving it with quite thin walls.

This depends of course upon the type of wood being used. Coarse-grained wood like oak and elm would be quite unsuitable for this thinning down treatment, but a hard, fine-grained variety such as boxwood, sycamore, rosewood, or beech, is completely amenable.

121. Decorating the container with black lines made by the heat of a length of fine wire stretched across and held down on the surface of the wood and positioned in slight nicks already made with the point of a skew chisel.

The next operation, if allowed for, is to start the final parting off of the container from its fixings on the lathe, remembering to leave room to clear any screw points that may be there. Then, before complete parting off, the container is finish-sanded.

A little decoration may be an improvement, and an easy and attractive form of this is to burn lines around the container, say one each side close to the join of the lid, and one at the base. First, score the position of the lines by a gentle application of the point of a skew chisel while the wood is revolving. A length of fine wire held between both hands is used for the scorching process. The middle of the wire is positioned from above to fit down into the score marks, pressed down each side by the hands and held until the increasing friction causes the wire to heat up and burn its way into the wood. It gets quite hot in the process so use a piece of wire at least 8″ long! Excessive scorching each side of the score line is removed by further papering. After finishing and polishing, the final parting off operation completes the job.

No attempt should be made to remove the lid from the container immediately it has been finished, as the interior heat generated by sanding and polishing will prevent this, and the container should be put aside to 'cool down'. A day may not be too long!

Once the lid has been prised loose, the interior can be 'eased' by sanding and waxing so that the lid is an easier, although still tight, fit. Containers with lids made by this method always seem to retain their firm quality of 'fit', however long in use.

It should be obvious, but I will stress that only fully dry wood must be used in the first place!

Before experience is gained, it is almost certain that a beginner will make the interior of a container just too large so that his lid is too loose fitting for friction to hold it in. Then any attempt to work on the lid is defeated, as at the first touch of a tool it flies off the lathe into limbo. One way out is to bring up the revolving tail-centre as support so that the lid is kept on by its pressure. To avoid damage to the lid by the point of the revolving centre, a tiny hardboard disc is inserted between it and the lid. The lid can then be finished, except for the small area covered by the hardboard disc, and this bit will have to be done by hand, and serve you right!

Deep Containers

Without some special equipment, such as a small rest on a long swan-neck support that allows it to enter the interior of the container, very deep excavation is difficult and possibly hazardous, since the more an excavating tool protrudes over a normal rest, the more strain on the tool and the operator at the other end! Sometimes the rest can be inserted sideways on into the interior, giving closer support to the working edge of the tool, but it is all very difficult and not to be recommended to the beginner. There are a couple of safer ways of making deep containers.

They can be built up gradually, using 'collars' of wood, same or varied, each one anything up to 2″ thick. The first solid disc is fixed to the faceplate, turned to a round on the outside and hollowed on the face to make the bottom of the container. Another disc is then glued on to this, and when set firm, turned and hollowed to line up and merge with the first. This process is continued until the required size of container is obtained.

24. Hour-glasses

Two popular sizes of glass are shown in the photograph. The large one runs for an hour and the smaller for fifteen minutes. Glasses can be made and filled for any reasonable running time: tiny pulse-glasses used by hospital personnel, the well-known egg-timers, and monster showpieces of four-hour duration. Sand is chosen from four different colours, as well as the natural shade.

Hour-glass stands are made from hardwood, the best that can be obtained, but only very little is required. Those shown are of Cuban

122. Hour-glasses.

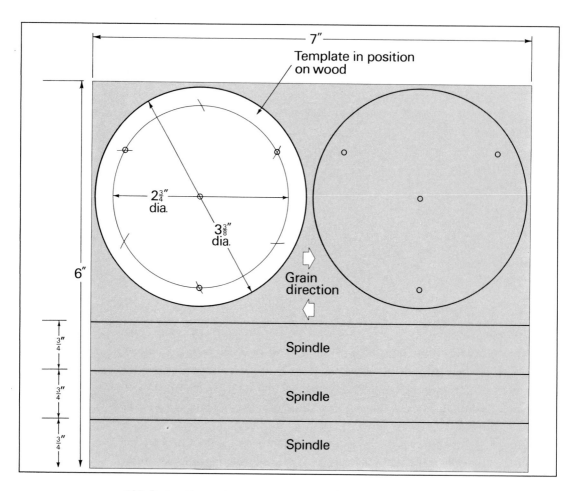

123. Parts of hour-glass.

mahogany from an old piece of furniture that was past restoring. An alternative to the traditional fine hardwoods is bleached pine which would go very well in modern kitchens. Another suitable wood is hornbeam.

The small dimensions of the various parts of both types of stand make for an easy project well within the capacity of the owner of a drill-driven lathe. I shall describe how to make a quarter-hour glass, but the method is the same for larger models.

A cardboard template is needed to start the job, and this is set out as shown in the drawing. Two concentric circles are described, the outside one of 3⅜″ diameter and the other of 2¾″. The inner circle is divided into six equal divisions by striking the compass around it at the same radius. Alternate divisions are pricked with an awl to give three points at 120 degrees. These will be the centres for the stand spindles.

The drawing shows that all the wood needed is taken from a piece 7″ long by 6″ wide and ¾″ thick. It makes an easier job if at least one face is planed and sanded smooth and the dimensions drawn out on that side. The template is laid on the work and two adjacent circles are drawn and the spindle centres marked. The exact centres for the screw-chuck are also marked through the template.

Bases are made roughly circular by sawing off the corners. The centre point is countersunk so that the work will 'bottom' flat and firm on the screw-chuck. A screw-chuck is the handiest fixing device for turning the bases, but one may not be available on a drill-driven lathe. An alternative is to fix a scrap of wood on the faceplate, turn it down, mark a $3\frac{3}{8}''$ circle and prick the positions of spindle centres through the template. After it has been marked to ensure that it will go back in the same position, this false faceplate is removed and small holes are drilled through the spindle centre marks. Screws through these holes will secure the base to the false faceplate. The assembly is then refixed to the metal faceplate.

The edge of the base is turned down with a $\frac{3}{8}''$ gouge to the template size, finished with a sharp, flat scraper, then beaded and shaped with any suitable tool.

The outside face can be patterned with a flat scraper, but the decoration must be below the surface so that when the hour-glass is upturned it will stand firm. After sanding smooth, a coat of sealer is applied with a cloth and gently dried by friction. The work is lightly sanded again, then a touch of white friction polish is applied, followed by wax. The base is then removed from the lathe and the operation repeated with the other base.

Spindles are fixed with dowels, so holes $\frac{1}{4}''$ diameter and about $\frac{1}{4}''$ deep are drilled in relevant positions on the inner faces of the bases. Holes are also drilled in the centres to take the hour-glass caps (preferably using a $\frac{1}{2}''$ or $\frac{3}{4}''$ Forstner Bit).

These faces can then be polished by hand (very little will show anyway in the finished stand) or pressed into a temporary wooden holding chuck for polishing on the lathe. The recess in a home-made chuck should not provide too tight a fit for the base lest it damages polished surfaces. It should be made very slightly on the loose side and packed out with newspaper which will give a good enough grip for the job.

When the spindles have been cut from the block of wood, the first is put between centres and turned down to a cylinder $\frac{1}{2}''$ diameter for most of its length measuring from the tailstock end. Since the wood is only $\frac{3}{4}''$ square to start with, there is the possibility that the driving centre might split it so you must take the precaution of helping the spurs to bite by first sawing a shallow cut across the end of the wood.

Calipers are used to measure the exact distance between the two hour-glass end caps, this measurement being marked on the spindle starting from the tailstock end. End-cap dimensions determine the length of

124. Copy of an old five-spindle hour-glass in ivory and mahogany. A template was essential for the spindles and bases. The glass insert is modern, being blown complete. Its old counterpart was in two separate bulbs that had to be joined in the middle with a securing band. A wafer thin disc of ivory had to be recessed into the bases. For this, part of a tusk was used, cut 'across' in order to obtain maximum diameter. This shows a tiny nerve channel in the centre. The spindle ends had to be made from sawn chunks of ivory, turned roughly round between centres and then held at one end in a Burnerd self-centring chuck to hold them for turning into completed knobs before parting off. Both spindles and knobs were tapped to take short lengths of threaded brass rod. Ivory turns well, provided the tools are very frequently sharpened, and patience is used as well as skill. No finishing is needed, apart from burnishing with cloth. It has a delicate grain of its own which is too fine to be seen in the photograph.

dowels which fix spindles, so these measurements are also marked off. The spindle centre is marked also and it is then taken off the lathe. The other two spindles are place between the centres and turned down to ½″ diameter, the first then being used as a guide to mark them so that all measurements are identical.

Spindles can be turned to whatever design is required, the positions of any beads being marked and cut first with the parting tool, and curves formed with a small, sharp gouge. If you use a chisel for this the thin stock is liable to whip and develop ribs. Beads are rounded off with a ¼″ chisel or sharp parting tool and the dowels at each end of the spindle turned down to ¼″ diameter. The first spindle should be completed, and then the other two turned as copies, all centres being retained so that alterations can be made to any one if it does not conform to the other. (Many excellent designs emanate from the accidental slip of a tool!) When spindles are identical they are sanded and polished and the waste parted off at the driving spur end.

A spot of glue is let into each of the six spindle holes in the bases and either electricians' rubber grommets or cut foam plastic 'washers' fitted into the cap holes. It would be an advantage to have three hands for holding spindles, hour-glass and bases in place, but the normal human can effect accurate assembly with a little patience! A weight on top will hold the completed assembly until the glue sets.

25. Table Lighters

Making the wooden bodies to contain the metal cups of the lighter inserts demonstrates two more 'tricks of the trade'; a method of holding half-finished work on a tapered spigot mandrel, and the complete removal of all sign of screw-holes combined with a good finish to the bases.

Wood about ½″ thicker than the depth of the metal cup is required, and this is mounted on a small faceplate with screws. An ⅛″ penetration of three screws into the wood should prove ample fixing. It is turned to a true

125. Table lighters.

disc and the front faced, all with the long and strong ⅜″ gouge. The hole to take the metal cup can be formed either with the beading and parting tool completely, or a drill of slightly less diameter used first and widened out with the parting tool, or if you are lucky to have one, a saw tooth machine centre drill of exactly the right diameter required—this saves time and work. The wood is then turned and finished to the required design and removed from the faceplate.

Scrap wood, either on a faceplate or screw-chuck, is turned down to a short tapered plug or spigot of a diameter enabling the wooden lighter body to be jammed on by pushing the hole for the cup on to it. The secret of a good friction hold of wood to wood is the *very slight* taper of the spigot. To ensure that the lighter body is not jammed on 'out of true' a series of pencil lines ⅟16″ apart is made on the spigot by revolving it and holding a pencil point against it. Tapping the body with the side of the clenched fist should be the only force needed to fix the body firmly on and parallel to one of the pencil lines.

The base can now be cleaned up with the gouge, entering on its side and cutting with a slight arc cut to the centre. All traces of screw holes can be removed and the base scraped, sanded and polished. The enthusiast can decorate the base with a small pointed scraper tool, but in any event it should be tested with a straightedge for flatness, or slight concavity before removing from the plug, to ensure that it stands firm.

26. Table Napkin Rings

The wood for these is held in the clamp-ring chuck in this case, and it is my practice to use sufficient length, with waste allowance, to produce either two or three rings. Endeavouring to make more in one setting up is likely to give trouble with vibration and wood turning 'out of true' because of no support at one end.

A cylinder is made by using the roughing down gouge, then a drill is placed in the tailstock and the cylinder drilled as far as possible in one go. A saw tooth bit of large diameter—say 1½"—is the easiest and quickest way, or else a smaller diameter hole drilled with whatever is available and widened out to finished size by using the skew scraper as in turned box making. After this has been done the exterior diameter of the cylinder is reduced to whatever finished size required. Here again we have the principle of retaining as much wood as possible *before* drilling out, *then* reducing by removing waste from the outside diameter. This makes for truer holes, and less risk of bursting out thin walls.

The bored cylinder is marked out from the end to length of first napkin ring, and the mark scored deeply with the point of a small skew chisel. Any beading, shaping, or decorative work is done, and the beading and parting tool is ideal for this, the outside of the ring is sanded and polished, the inside best left sanded.

The napkin ring is then parted completely off down the waste side of the skew chisel score mark, and you can play hoop-la by catching the ring on your finger as it leaves the rest of the cylinder. The partly finished ring is used as a template to mark off for the next, and so on until two or three have been made.

126. Table napkin rings.

There should be enough waste left of the cylinder to turn down to a stub spigot as in the making of the table lighter. One by one the napkin rings are jammed on this stub so that the raw edges left by parting off can be shaped, cleaned up and polished.

27. The Art of Decorating Wood by Burning

Pokerwork and Pyrography are both terms meaning burning marks into wood and other materials, using all sorts of tools ranging from the heated common nail to complicated electrical machines. Even the heat of the sun directed through a magnifying glass has been used successfully.

My late friend Edward Pinto in his book, *Treen and Other Wooden Bygones*, lists the art under the description 'Incised Surface Decoration', and states: 'Patterns made with a heated steel point are known as pokerwork; if the work is fine and used to create a hot etched picture, it is termed pyrography.' Another book of his, *Tunbridge and Scottish Souvenir Woodware*, includes some marvellous examples of the artistic skill of the 19th century, achieved with only the primitive tools available then.

The Child family has been interested in this craft for many years now, specialising mainly in wood as the 'canvas' for pictures and designs, and occasionally experimenting with leather. Favourite woods are sycamore, lime, holly, whitewood, fine quality birch plywood, and maple.

A hard, close-grained white surface brings out fine detailed work to best advantage—softer woods fuzz the burn, but even so the general effect can still be most attractive. The wood can act simply as a plain base for a picture, or pyrography can be used as a decoration—for example, on a tray.

Factory machine-sanded surfaces are not as clean and fine as they appear, and where possible this surface should be scraped to a polished finish. For large areas a Record Cabinet scraper is the ideal tool.

In the beginning we preferred a fine hard white wood which was completely free of any blemish, with no grain markings, and as near as we could get to a white parchment paper. Then, as techniques improved, we found we could use faulty timber to very good effect—grain marking

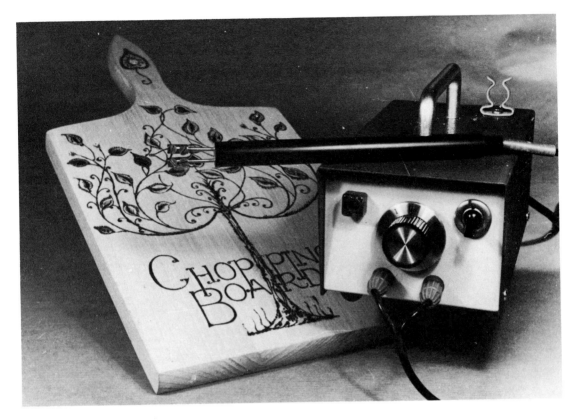

127. The machine designed by Roy Child for decorating wood.

became clouds, and small knots were incorporated into tree trunks in country scenes. The latest machine we now manufacture is capable of meeting the requirements of the most professional of artists, and also takes the simplest work in its stride—including lettering, house-names, signatures, and repetition branding. It is very safe in use, and many schools now have them for the kids as a 'fun-tool'—much more interesting than crayons!

For design work a variety of different shaped nibs, easily fitted and cheap to replace, are supplied with the machine, as well as additional wire that can be formed with fine nosed pliers into customised shapes, brands, and initials. Designs can be traced on to the wood surface, or sketched in with pencil. A simple project would be a set of table mats from cork-backed birch plywood.

Pictures

For economy, my son Chris uses fine sycamore veneer sheet glued to a hardboard back. The finished picture is then glued to a larger piece of ½″

128. The simplest of wood objects can be made very attractive—decorated wooden spoons and chopping boards are very popular.

plywood. The exposed surfaces of the plywood backing are mitre veneered with burr walnut. The back is chamfered all round to remove the heavy look, then stained brown and finished off with a coat of cellulose sanding sealer. The picture and surrounding veneer is given a coat of Rustins Clear Plastic, a finish that can be brought up to clear glass perfection, or steel wool is applied until a velvet matt finish is obtained. My daughter Patricia's pictures are usually framed, glass-covered or not depending on her choice.

Trays

Some of her larger works are made into trays, or set into table tops, or made into fireplace screens. If sufficient margin is left around the drawing, an edging border can be simulated by cutting lightly all round with a marking knife, with additional mitre-cuts at the corners. Then a metal straightedge is lined up $\frac{1}{16}''$ *over* the knife cuts, hiding them under the metal. With a knotted cloth suitable stain is applied sparingly right up to the straightedge, which is then carefully removed. It will be found that the stain has seeped under the straightedge, and is stopped clean by the knife cut. You will then almost certainly be admired for the cleanness and accuracy of the 'veneered' surround.

Buttons and Hanging Plates

Margaret excels in drawing in the round. Her buttons are turned from ¼″ by 1″ diameter boxwood. A metal faceplate is protected by a scrapwood disc, and the boxwood roughly sawn to 1½″ diameter, fixed by double-sided adhesive tape to the centre. The back of the button is turned to finished outside diameter 1⅜″, and a small central recess made for the metal fixing tab. The button is then reversed, centred, and given its front design. Roy does all this with a set of his miniature gouges and scrapers. My wife Margaret has to use an optician's lupe, and eye-strain is not uncommon after a long spell of etching.

For the round wall plaques or plates we first used sycamore 1¼″ thick so that we could screw it to a faceplate and get a deep enough saucer recess in the front without the danger of fouling the fixing screws. Now by employing the screwless chuck (see page 133), we can use ¾″ or even thinner stock and get the same result. The sawn 12″ diameter disc is screwed to the faceplate with screws that enter the wood no deeper than ⅜″. A 1/16″ deep recess is turned in the centre 5″ diameter to take the screwless chuck fitting, and the rest of the wood is rounded off like the base of a saucer. The surface is sanded, stained, and shellac-sander sealed, then the faceplate removed, the chuck fitted so that the wood is reversed when replaced on the lathe.

The recess for the drawing is about 7″ diameter and first notched in to depth required by using a common parting tool scraper-fashion. The majority of the inner waste is then removed with a HSS bowl gouge, followed by a heavy-duty dome-shaped scraper, and then cleaned up further with a high speed steel scraper bar. Margaret prefers a dead flat or slightly domed surface. Then the outside rim of the recess is curved inward from the plate edge, to end in a rim round the recess 1/16″ proud of it.

After sanding, this outside rim is stained brown by using a knot of cloth dipped into the stain and applied from the outside edge toward the recess, the lathe run at lowest speed.

Despite the sparing use of the stain, and the most careful approach, it is almost certain that a little will overlap the rim and get on to the surface of the recess. This is cleaned away by using the scraper bar to remove just enough wood to get down to an unstained surface and leave a clean, sharp edge.

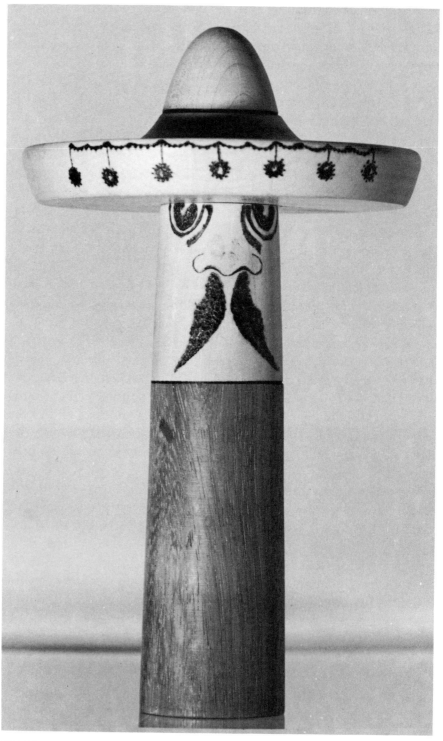

129. Merry Bandidos.

Additional Decoration

We have a souvenir plate from Germany in our collection. It has a central picture, and the outside rim is filled in by the coats of arms of various towns. Enamel paints have been used to colour in these arms. A less crude application is by use of leather dyes, which can produce various shades of colour in chosen parts of the pyrography. For practice a beginner could use a simple Painting-by-Numbers project.

Ornaments

All woodworkers acccumulate odds and ends of nice wood—too small for serious use, but too good to throw away. For example, assume a length of dark wood $4'' \times 2\frac{1}{2}'' \times 2\frac{1}{2}''$. This is turned to a cylinder and parted down at the headstock end to a dowel $1\frac{1}{2}''$ long $\times 1''$ diameter.

Some short lengths of whitewood are centrally bored with the grain right through with a $1''$ diameter hole, and then sliced up to give squares about $2'' \times 2'' \times 1''$ thick. This square is glued over the dowel, leaving $\frac{1}{2}''$ dowel still protruding, and the whole of the dark and white wood turned to a blunt cone.

A square of whitewood about $3'' \times 3''$ by $\frac{1}{2}''$ or $\frac{3}{4}''$ thick has another piece $1\frac{1}{2}'' \times 1\frac{1}{2}'' \times 1''$ glued to its centre. This is mounted by screwchuck, and with a $\frac{1}{2}''$ spindle gouge transformed into a sombrero hat. The screwhole is widened to $1''$ diameter and deep enough to accommodate the dowel left on the end of the cone. When assembled the hat is embellished with pyrography in wavy lines around the brim, and the white face is given two flashing eyes and a mustachio. We now have our mustachioed Merry Bandidos.

A selection of wood from the scrap pile can be transformed into long sad figures, short tubby smiling ones, and any family variety in between. My American friends will no doubt produce some charming tall-hatted Uncle Sams, and the Welsh a sinister group of witches!

A potter friend would find no difficulty in making the hats so then the ornament could perform as an ashtray.

28. Laminated and Checkered Woodturnery

This is interesting work and provides an alternative to turning from completely solid wood, offers opportunities for artistic design and contrast in colours, and the extra labour involved in the preparation and building up with small pieces of wood is offset by the saving of timber and time. There is also a considerable saving of time in finish-turning due to the absence of bulk waste in the centre.

Assembly and gluing up of the segments can now be achieved quickly, easily and efficiently by using an ingenious patented circular cramp. The 'Flexicramp' consists of a band of spring steel combined with a tensioning cramp performing the dual purpose of adjusting the diameter to the size of work required, and tightening in a fine adjustment for gluing up. Provided that the blocks used are accurately cut for angle and are of uniform thickness in each assembled ring, then use of the cramp and suitable glue ensures a safe assembly of the whole ready for turning to the finished design.

Cutting Angle

A simple arrangement, say for a bowl, is a series of rings made up from an even number of blocks, and the rings are glued, one on top of the other, to produce the depth of bowl required. To find the angle to which the segments must be cut, the number of blocks per ring is divided into 360 and the answer again divided by two. For twelve segments the calculation would be 360 divided by twelve, giving 30, dividing again by 2, giving 15, and 15 degrees is the angle required.

130. A selection of built-up turnery. The multi-coloured bowls were constructed of sycamore, guarea and circassian walnut and have striking contrast to the bowl on the left made from plain deal.

Methods of Cutting

Any of the following:
- (a) Home-made mitre block.
- (b) Commercial saw especially made for mitre and angle cutting—e.g. Ulmia machine.
- (c) Circular and radial cutting power saws provided with an angle-cutting fence and adjustable stop.

Whichever method is used, accuracy is essential as only glue holds the assembly together, and for safety as well as a professional finish and appearance there must be no gaps between the gluing surfaces. There is no need to get an immaculately smooth finish on the ends of the blocks since the slightly roughened finish from a sharp saw gives an excellent gluing 'key'. A useful home-made taper gauge is easily made up for testing the segments for correct angle.

Making Up

The test of good workmanship is to assemble one layer in the Flexicramp *dry*, tighten up and hold to the light to ensure that there are no gaps. If light comes through anywhere—there are!

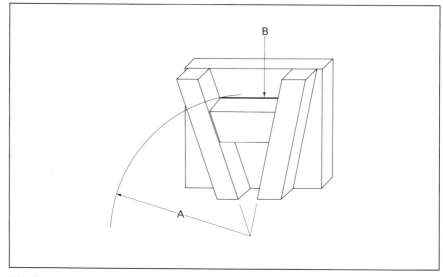

131. Taper gauge.
A simple taper gauge made from two strips of wood and plywood for testing that the included angle of the blocks is correct and that they are dimensionally accurate and will fit within very close limits to the radius of the disc (A), indicated by the pencil line 'B'.

In addition to the correct cutting angle, the segments in any one layer have to be identical in thickness. Running the wood lengths through a planing machine equipped with a thicknessing attachment is one way of ensuring this, or if the segments have already been cut, a simple planing jig can be just as efficient.

Method of Assembly

1. Set up blocks in order of pattern required and coat with glue.
2. Put first layer in Flexicramp and coat the top with glue.
3. Lay subsequent layers on top, coating each layer with glue.
4. Drop in the base and use a distance piece of flexible tubing around it to centralise it.
5. Tighten up the Flexicramp by screwing up the handle.

A light hammer can be used to tap the blocks into position back against the band of the cramp as each block is laid.

To make sure that each assembled and glued layer is firmly in contact with its neighbours an end-pressure clamp can be devised from a backing board and two or three large G-clamps. When these are in position, the Flexicramp can be withdrawn by unscrewing it into parts and is then immediately available for use when reassembled. The glued-up assembly should not be touched again until the glue is really set, and a delay of 24 hours is not too long to wait.

132. Blocks which are not cut from specially prepared timber strip must be levelled down to the same thickness for each layer in this simple trough shaped jig with a plane. Make sure that the first and last blocks in the line are of equal thickness, and keep each layer separate.

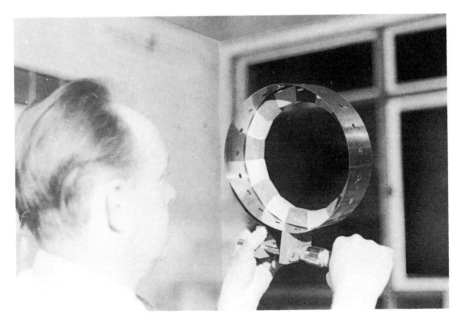

133. Before you glue up, assemble a ring of blocks in the Flexicramp and hold it up to the light to make sure that there are no visible gaps.

134. This jig enables the blocks to be set out in patterns as they will appear in the finished work and also allows the edges to be glued to be coated with glue in one operation.

135. The disc is assembled 'upside down' to prevent the glue from running on to the base so the wide blocks go in last. It may be necessary to slacken off the Flexicramp slightly to get the last block in.

136. The plywood base is dropped into position. This is best made about 1″ smaller in diameter than the disc to save turning, and the disc should be centralised by using a piece of plastic tubing as a distance piece.

137. End-pressure may be effectively applied using G cramps and a cramping board. Note the aluminium sheet to prevent the work adhering to the board and the plastic tubing to centralise the base. Large G cramps can be balanced by placing them on both sides of the work.

Bases

Plywood is recommended for these since there is a possibility of solid wood, however dry and seasoned, still 'moving' at a later date and causing the segment joints to open up under its pressure. Plywood, by nature of its construction, is much more stable. A good idea is to cut the circular bases about 1″ less in diameter than the segment layers, and centralise the base on the bottom by inserting round it a distance piece made out of flexible tubing fitting between base and side of the cramp. This saves a lot of turning, and a neat appearance can be given to the inside bottom of the bowl by rebating with a parting tool to form a slight step from the inside of curve of the bowl to the base.

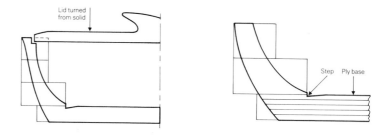

138. The method of forming a rebate from the built-up work to the plywood base is clearly shown in the lower picture where it will be seen that the plywood face is slightly shelved off to remove traces of inlay. The top sketch shows the method of rebating the turned disc to fit a lid to make a workbox.

Turning to Finished Shape

A bowl-turning speed of about 700 r.p.m. is amply sufficient. High speeds do not help as much as sharp tools, and a low but efficient speed is much better, especially from the safety point of view.

Segmented work is best not turned down to a thin wall, so attempting to bring down to a thickness of under 3/8″ is not advisable. The work should be stopped frequently for inspection in case any faults in construction appear, and it would be unwise to carry on turning if there is. Wearing a face shield is a precaution against injury in the event of disintegration. When turning a cylinder between centres—say a biscuit barrel, additional support should be given to the open end by using a disc of scrapwood running on the tail centre.

29. Variations of Turnery

Twist Turnings

Once the lathe has been used to round the stock, leaving a plain cylinder, taper, or combination of squares and rounds, then it ceases to have an active part in the production of twist or spiral turnery and becomes a vice, a convenient holder of the wood so as to enable the carpentry work to be done. This is the fashioning of the twist, or bines, and it is all hand work.

There is a special sort of lathe used in industry, a combination of metal screwcutting machine and woodturning lathe that is capable of producing a machined twist turning; work that cannot be done automatically by the normal wood lathe. A twist is a variety of quick pitch thread and the lathe would need a tool carrier to move rapidly along the bed and cut the thread. The only way to do this manually is to mark out the lines of the twist on the wood with pencil and start by cutting down on the lines with a tenon saw equipped with a depth guide. The waste wood has then to be removed by chiselling, rasping and papering. Not really a turner's job.

Oval Turnings

This can be done completely by the lathe, and is comparatively simple. The initial stock used has to be accurately sawn rectangular wood that is longer than the finished work by say 2″, and with the size of the rectangle just a trifle larger than the required oval finish. The ends of the stock are marked for centre, but not by drawing the usual diagonal lines from corner to corner. Instead, the lines are drawn as shown in the photograph, and in addition they are extended along the length of the stock and join up. A compass is then set by experiment to draw the two arcs shown and this will determine the position of two more 'centre' marks on the *short* axis of the

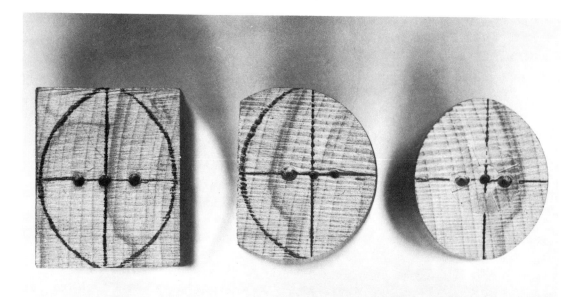

139. End markings for oval turnings.

bisecting lines. So we now have a set of three 'centres', with an identical set at the other end of the stock. The wood is set up in the lathe between either the left- or right-hand pair of 'off-centres'. The wood will turn parallel but out of true rotation and this may cause some lathe vibration. It is important that the hand-rest is placed so that when the lathe is revolved by hand one or more complete turns, the wood does not collide with it at any point.

The turning is done with the roughing out gouge placed on the rest clear of the revolving wood and pushed forward until contact is made and small shavings start to come off. Then it can be traversed back and forth, but not to the full length of the wood, leaving a small amount of waste full-sized at either end. The lathe has to be stopped at frequent intervals to inspect progress and wood removal continues until one pencil line is reached, then the stock is removed, set up again on its other pair of 'off-centres' and the process repeated, until the other pencil line is reached. The reason for leaving some waste at each end is so that the gouge does not remove any of the 'centre' points. The final job is to set up the completed oval on its pair of true centres and skim off the pencil lines with one or two passes of the roughing out gouge. After papering (slowest lathe speed), the work can be shaped and parted off.

Cabriole-type Legs

These turnings are again accomplished by the use of 'off-centre' techniques. The stock is set up between true centres and turned to a cylinder with the roughing down gouge. Then, at the tailstock end, a new 'centre' is marked at a point halfway between true centre and the edge of the cylinder. At the headstock end another 'centre' is made only a slight (almost negligible) distance from true centre and directly opposite in line from the one at the tailstock. When set up on these new 'centres' the wood at the headstock end will revolve only slightly out of true revolution, but this will be very much pronounced at the tailstock. The rest should be positioned carefully to clear the work at all times. When the lathe is switched on, the eccentric rotation of the wood throws out two distinct shadow cones—this can more easily be seen if there is a light at the other side of the lathe bed. There will be a light shadow, more pronounced than the dark one, at the tailstock, and gradually reducing to an intersection with dark shadow at the headstock. A ½″ spindle-nosed gouge is a good tool with which to start shaping. Point of entry about 1″ from the tailstock, gouge on the rest on its side (flute facing left) and pushed forward gently until contact is made with the revolving wood. The cut is made by twisting the gouge over on to its back, i.e. flute coming uppermost. The next cut is made from the other direction, as in forming a hollow.

By removing waste alternately this way from both sides, the hollow is gradually deepened until its bottom has disposed of all the light shadow and the wood at that point has been turned completely round.

If the lathe is stopped it will be seen that the club foot has been formed at the right of the hollow. Using a ¾″ roughing down gouge, the remainder of the light shadow cone is removed right up to the point near the headstock where it merges into dark.

The leg is then set up between its true centres again and the bottom of the club toe turned and finished.

A true cabriole leg is a cabinet-making job and usually started with a bandsaw or bowsaw to cut out to rough shape. The turner's job is just to do the foot.

Split Turnings

One method is to complete a full turning from solid stock and cut it into halves or quarters with a saw, but the waste of the saw kerf reduces the size of the finished items. A better way is to prepare the two or four lengths of stock and glue them together for turning in one piece, then to split them apart when the turning and polishing has been completed. The 'glue-and-brown paper' joint is excellent for the purpose. Another method is to use

140. Home-made jig for spoon turning.

strong tape now available 'sticky' on both sides. Another glue which will hold well is old-fashioned Cow gum, but this must be allowed to set. It is easily forced apart again using a thin chisel to start the separation and leverage does the rest. The set gum can be rolled off the wood with the fingers, leaving the original clean surface.

A four-prong driving centre is much preferred to the two-prong for this work, but the centre point of either must be an easy fit into the wood, or its pressure can split the segments during the turning process. At the tailstock end, a ring centre should be employed.

Pairs of sugar or salad spoons can be made by the split method, and the photograph shows a home-made jig whereby the bowl is held in a scrap wood hollow by a strap across the handle so that a round-nosed scraper can be used to hollow out the spoon cavity.

PART III

APPENDIX

30. Timber for Turning

It is too general to say that turners mostly use hardwoods and not softwoods. Roughly, softwoods come from coniferous trees like fir, pine and spruce. Hardwoods are mainly broadleaved trees of which examples are walnut, oak and mahogany. Parana pine turns well. It is a softwood. Yew is magnificent, and technically this is a softwood too. Balsa is almost useless and it is a hardwood. So any advice, unless sufficiently detailed to take up a whole book by itself, tends to bewilder rather than help. The best thing is to stick a piece of it between centres and if a *good finish* can be obtained then add it to your own list of suitable turning woods.

Seasoning

Another book is needed for this, but a rough guide is that imported hardwoods are likely to be drier than our home-grown variety. After all, they have to come a long way before we get them and this takes time. They could also have been kiln dried, which is a quick artificial seasoning process, but a lot of it is only air dried in plank, and this can take up to a year for every inch of thickness. Home seasoning by turners of timber in the round (in the log form) is a hit-or-miss process. The heartwood almost invariably cracks and the home turner is usually only able to handle logs of relatively small diameter, so that if they are sawn 'through and thorough' into planks, disposing of the heart, it reduces the timber left to only small section stuff. Timber most dependable for turnery without warping should have a moisture content of under 10%.

Sources of Timber for the Turner

Retail shops, builder's merchants, and small timber supply firms are not very likely sources for the relatively large lumps of hardwood we turners

Names of some Woods for Turnery Use

Acacia, African blackwood, African mahogany, African walnut, afrormosia, afzelia (doussie), agba, amboyna, American walnut, ash.

Beech, birch, blackbean, box, Brazilian walnut (Imbuia).

Chin chan, coachwood, cocobolo, coigue beech, coubard, Cuban mahogany.

Danta

Ebony, elm

Fruitwoods (apple, cherry, pear)

Greenheart

Hickory, holly, hornbeam

Iroko, Jelutong

Lacewood (plane), laurel, lignum vitae, lime

Mansonia, maple

Oak, olivewood

Panga panga, purpleheart

Ramin, rauli, rosewood

Sapele, sepetir, silky oak, sweet chestnut, sycamore

Tasmanian myrtle, teak

Utile

Walnut, wenge

Yew

Zebrano

need. They mainly deal in timber for joinery and carcassing work. The large timber supply firms who can cater for our requirements usually advertise well in trade journals and it is a question of looking for them. But perhaps they are too large to bother about our small demands, and also, if they are some distance away, the carriage costs can exceed the value of the wood ordered.

Small *sawmills* used to abound in most areas. Sadly now, mostly for economic reasons, they are being closed down, but those that are left have all got telephones. The business part of the telephone directory can point the finger at them, and the references of our public libraries can help as well. These mills produce fenceposts, coffin planks, farming timbers, mine tunnel supports, etc., and carry stocks of home-grown hardwoods, beech, elm, oak, sycamore, ash, some acacia, yew, walnut, cherry, lime. A lot of them obtain their wood by clearing farmers' land, felling trees that are in the way of new ditches, farm roads, barn sites. They usually have to contract to clear all the area, even if they have no immediate use for some of the trees growing on it. It is well worth while to seek out these small concerns and call on the owners; if possible make the acquaintance of the sawyer. Small 'shorts' of timber, hard and dry, may well be lying around. I have spotted some beautiful chunks used as chocks for machinery, and a softwood replacement made no difference. All the wood is sawn, but turners seldom need planed and squared stock. It may not be too dry, but the turner can take it home and stack it himself for future use.

You may be near a joinery works and can ask for offcuts. A piece turned, polished, and presented as an example of what these 'worthless' bits can be fashioned into, can well result in a lasting friendly relationship!

Boat builders and yards use a lot of hardwood, useful contacts for turners who live near the sea or the rivers.

Finally, there are firms who advertise and specialise in supplying 'wood for turners'. The objection is that one has to be nearby to see what is being offered, or trust that the firm really knows what we want, have it sent and pay the carriage costs. This can be most expensive.

31. Converting Your Own Timber

Many years ago, when tradesmen worked long hours but at a leisurely pace and enjoyed it, I visited the saw-mill. Huge logs were fed slowly lengthways into a vertical saw-blade which went majestically up and down, a mechanical version of the more arduous pit-saw days. There was a frightening bang when metal met metal buried in the wood, and the steam engine motor was thrown into neutral. The old saw doctor came out of his hut, shook his head sorrowfully, and went to work. A convenient time for tea-break, and then back to earning the daily bread. Nowadays, I believe bandsaws work at nearly supersonic speed, and the results of meeting a metal object can be quite devastating. Sawmills are then reluctant to accept customers' logs for conversion into planks, and I believe they have good reason!

However, the amateur can do a satisfactory job for himself if he owns a chainsaw, and especially if he has the use of a bandsaw as well. For example, quite a small diameter log can be converted to valuable turnery discs with the least amount of waste. The diagram shows a log of 12" diameter cut into twelve-inch segments, which are then cut down the centre. The bark and sap wood is planed away from the top of the segments to provide a flat surface for the faceplate, and then the segment sawn into a disc. If a bandsaw is not available, the corners are roughly sawn off with the chainsaw. What is very important is to remove the pith as shown by the dotted lines, say by one inch. This will ensure that splits will not develop in the discs later on. If the discs are rough-turned with the least delay, and kept under cover with good air circulation, the likelihood of side cracks or 'checks' is remote. However, if some time is likely to elapse before this procedure, it would be wise to roll the discs, like a wheel, through a shallow tray of hot candle-wax. This will seal the sides of the disc, and slow down the drying out of this area, allowing the faces of the disc to dry out and season at an even rate. If rectangular lengths are required, e.g. chair legs etc., the ends of the wood pieces are dipped into the wax.

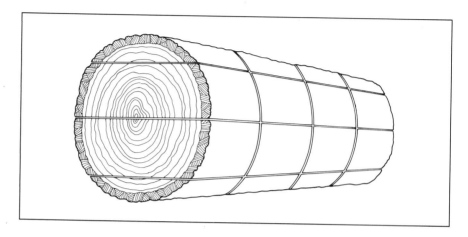

141a. Economic conversion of small-diameter logs

a) Saw log into segments the same length as the diameter of the log.
b) Saw segments down the centre into two pieces.
c) Plane or saw off bark and enough wood to leave a flat surface which will take a faceplate.
d) Band-saw segments into discs.
e) If unable to rough-turn for some time, roll sides of discs through a shallow tray of melted paraffin wax, so as to seal them from air.
f) When turning, reduce rim of bowl by at least ½" so that any pith (centre of wood) is removed. Failure to do this may lead to cracking.

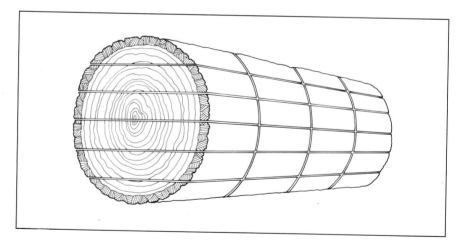

141b. Conversion of large-diameter logs
Proceed as above, but with more segments.

32. Turning Unseasoned Logs

It is well known that if timber is left for long in the round it is almost certain to develop cracks and shakes, most of them radiating from the centre pith. Anything turned from the log will crack this way sooner or later. We did some successful trials with polyethylene glycol (P.E.G.), immersing the partially turned logs in the solution, but this preparation has now become far too expensive for us. We economised by turning a large lamp base from an unseasoned, freshly-cut log. Then we applied a liberal coat of cellulose sanding sealer to the turned surface and this dried on well. When dry and hard, which takes a few hours (overnight is preferable), the sealer was lightly sanded, a pad of ooo steel wool applied, and then a final coat of Rustins Plastic Finish. Then we drilled as many large holes as deep as possible into the bottom of the lamp base, and filled them up with neat P.E.G. (like lard), then plugged the holes so that it would not leak out. We have examined this lamp closely over several months, and as yet there is no sign of warp or of any cracks. It is emphasised that the log chosen has to have the pith more or less centrally placed, that there must not be the slightest trace of cracks, or any ones on the outside of the log that cannot be turned completely away in the design.

Another project was a large base turned to a series of basins increasing in size from top to bottom, rather like an ornamental fountain where the water emerges from the top and overflows from basin to basin. Then we drilled a full 2″ diameter hole right down the centre to see if this was enough to eliminate cracking without the use of expensive P.E.G. A suitable plug for the top was to be made to take the bulb fitting. However, before this could be done, my wife Margaret impounded the base and it

142. The big lamp was turned from hornbeam, the interior drilled with a series of holes, filled with neat polyethylene and plugged. When signs of penetration of the P.E.G. were observed on the outside of the wood, the lamp was completely turned and finished. To date, no warping has occurred. The attractive eggholder is from an elm log with a large hole drilled through the centre. The vase is also elm with the interior almost completely hollowed out. The making of the bottle lamp is explained on page 182.

stands in the kitchen—full of fresh eggs. Very unusual, and I would suggest a very marketable design. The wooden egg atop conceals the hole.

On the theory that the more wood that could be removed from the interior of the base, the less likelihood there was of the remainder cracking, we turned a big diameter log into a lamp base, then drilled out the interior right through, leaving a wall not more than ¾″ thick overall. The idea was to let the wood dry out, incurring no cracks in the process, and then provide top and bottom wooden plugs to fit the now attractive oval shape. However, Margaret again took over, and the lamp base is now the holder of very attractive flower displays. Roy also suggested that if we turned the base upside down, inserted an interior light source that reflected on the ceiling, we could have some very successful subdued lighting effects.

33. Making Woodturnery Pay

Although the keen amateur turner should concern himself mainly with improving his techniques and finishing processes—progressing in stages and being able eventually to produce first-class results in all varieties of the craft, there is no reason why he should not in addition make some money from his efforts. To some, 'profit' is a dirty word, but even to them there should be no objection to earning sufficient remuneration to meet the *costs of production*, thereby providing enjoyment without financial strain.

The mere fact that one is able to sell work should convey a real sense of satisfaction in the proof that it is worth someone else's money. The beginner first starts with an attempt to please himself with what his skill has produced. If he ever does reach the stage of being completely satisfied, then, paradoxically, he falls short in his values, for no real craftsman achieves this stage. It will be far easier to please his 'nearest and dearest', to whom at first all is excellence that is presented from the workshop. Other relatives will be complimentary too, and, as knowledge of his new proficiency spreads, neighbours and acquaintances will all give praise in return for their gifts. However, it is the worker who should think upon the horse's mouth in some of these cases.

The situation becomes a great deal clearer when a complete stranger, perhaps a shop owner, sees the wares and offers to buy them. This conveys a good unsentimental appraisal of value, of far more use to the amateur than all of Aunt Nellie's gratuitous effervescence for her birthday gift. The opinion of a shopowner is especially worth while, since his job is to re-sell the products to the general and (sometimes) discerning public.

When the amateur has progressed to this stage then his ego has been given a tremendous boost, for he has been given convincing proof that his work has merit.

But how much merit? Before he can really believe his work is worthy of his labours, then he must know how to value his product. Most good amateurs venturing timidly into the cold world of commerce tend to err on the side of cheapness, not in quality, but in placing too low a monetary value on their work. This may not matter when the purpose is merely to support the expenses of the hobby, for then labour costs can be ignored, making the asking price ridiculously cheap in comparison to the equivalent commercial product.

Costing

This term can cover almost everything, down to the wear in shoeleather walking to and fro from the workshop, but there is seldom need to go this far. The manufacture of a fruit bowl of a given size can be an example, and the costs involved would include:

Materials Wood (cost delivered to workshop), abrasive papers, sealers, polishes, green cloth base.

Labour The time needed to convert the block of wood into a finished bowl ready for sale. This should be determined as accurately as possible, leaving nothing out. It may only take two minutes to affix the cloth base to one finished bowl and this may not be considered important until it is realised that it would take an hour to complete thirty.

It is difficult for the amateur to decide what to charge, per hour, for his labour, and one suggestion is to find out the local hourly rate paid to a semi-skilled woodworker, bearing in mind that he will be an employee, and possibly has partly-paid insurance benefits, tool allowance, holiday pay, etc., in addition.

However, one has to start somewhere and this seems as good a method as any. Some years ago I was given the job of turning a bulbous wooden pedestal used in the production of reproduction furniture. I had never turned one before so I set the workshop clock for costing purposes. The cabinet-maker supplied his own timber, so the cost was labour only, and it worked out a x-value. Today I still do this work for very little more than x-value and the cabinet-maker is a satisfied and regular customer. What he perhaps does not realise is that now I can easily do three of the turnings in the same time as I did one in the beginning, so the 'semi-skilled rate' has automatically risen to the 'fully-skilled'. MATERIALS and LABOUR together are items *directly* related to the manufacture of the fruit bowl—in other words the FLAT COST.

Overheads These are the expenses of a workshop which cannot be directly allocated to the making of the fruit bowl and yet are a necessary part of its production. Examples are rent, electricity, heating, rates, depreciation, maintenence (machines, tool sharpening, workshop cleaning), book-keeping, etc.

The amateur, in his own home and workshop, doing his small amount of paperwork in the evenings, may be inclined to regard the addition of a percentage of overheads to the fruit bowl as insignificant and too difficult to work out anyway, but even very small firms would soon be out of business if they ignored these expenses. A fairly easy 'guessway' would be to add a small percentage charge on to MATERIALS or LABOUR cost. With this, at least some idea will be obtained of the total cost of production.

The FLAT COST, plus the percentage of OVERHEADS, will be the full cost of making the fruit bowl, and this cost, at least, has to be recovered before the amateur is in business proper.

A far more accurate method of determining this amount is not by costing one bowl as described, but by timing the total cost of, say, 12 similar bowls, and dividing the result by 12. Every piece of wood is not identical to the next, the operation is spread over a considerable period and not in just one concerted attempt, so the average figure obtained is much more likely to be a more accurate one. There is no need, nor is it recommended, that the worker starts on a dozen bowls and does nothing else until they are finished. What is important is that every minute of time spent on a dozen is recorded.

Profit

This is the jam on the bread, and the full cost, plus margin of profit, is the worker's selling price of his product. What amount he adds as profit is his own affair and the more he gets the better off he will be. There is the small matter of COMPETITION to consider. To attempt to sell 'too dear' is almost as bad as 'too cheap'. A good guide is to price a similar product displayed in shops that specialise in woodware. The shopowner also has to make a living, so at least one third has to be deducted from the price in the window to obtain some idea of what the article was sold to the shop for. In addition, there will be some sort of percentage of SALES TAX which has also to be deducted from the shop's retail price of the item.

There is nothing wrong in the amateur selling his work direct to the public and not through shops. So he can have two prices for the same article, a lower one to the shop, and a higher figure if he sells direct to his customer. The nearer the latter figure is to the 'shop price' the more extra jam for the amateur, and in addition, he will not be setting up in unfair competition with the shop owner.

'One-off' Jobs

With the march towards huge combines and more and more mass-production techniques, the individual specialist craftsman is now a comparative rarity and can be much in demand for small jobs in which the big firms are simply not interested.

Antique dealers, cabinet-makers, repairers and restorers are always on the look out for the 'little man' who can be relied upon when odd knobs are required, or some antique piece needs a turned replacement. They can often be persuaded to supply their own wood for the job, and then the amateur has only to set his clock and time his labour. It is universally recognised that 'one-off' jobs need thinking about, more time in setting up, and greater concentration than repetitive work, so the amateur *doing a good job* can price it accordingly.

Metric Conversion Table

Inches	Millimetres
1/32	0.8
1/16	1.6
1/8	3.2
3/16	4.8
1/4	6.4
5/16	7.9
3/8	9.5
7/16	11.1
1/2	12.7
9/16	14.3
5/8	15.9
11/16	17.5
3/4	19.1
13/16	20.6
7/8	22.2
15/16	23.8
1	25.4
2	50.8
3	76.2
4	101.4
5	127.0
6	152.4
7	177.5
8	203.2
9	228.6
10	254.0
11	279.5
12	304.8
18	457.2
24	609.6
36	914.4

INDEX